Rich Dad's

THE BUSINESS SCHOOL

SECOND EDITION

FOR PEOPLE WHO LIKE HELPING PEOPLE

Other bestselling books
by Robert T. Kiyosaki with Sharon L. Lechter
in the Rich Dad Series:

Rich Dad Poor Dad
What The Rich Teach Their Kids About Money That The Poor And Middle Class Do Not

Rich Dad's CASHFLOW Quadrant
Rich Dad's Guide To Financial Freedom

Rich Dad's Guide to Investing
What The Rich Invest In That The Poor And Middle Class Do Not

Rich Dad's Rich Kid Smart Kid
Give Your Child A Financial Head Start

Rich Dad's Retire Young Retire Rich
How To Get Rich Quickly And Stay Rich Forever

Rich Dad's Prophecy
Why The Biggest Stock Market Crash In History Is Still Coming…
And How You Can Prepare Yourself And Profit From It!

Rich Dad's Success Stories
Real Life Success Stories from Real Life People
Who Followed the Rich Dad Lesson

Rich Dad's Guide to Becoming Rich
Without Cutting Up Your Credit Cards
Turn "Bad Credit" into "Good Credit"

Rich Dad's Who Took My Money?
Why Slow Investors Lose and Fast Money Wins

Rich Dad Dad Poor Dad for Teens
The Secrets About Money—That You Don't Learn in School!

Rich Dad's Before You Quit Your Job
10 Real-Life Lessons Every Entrepreneur Should Know About
Building A Multimillion-Dollar Business

Rich Dad's

THE BUSINESS SCHOOL

SECOND EDITION

FOR PEOPLE WHO LIKE HELPING PEOPLE

By Robert T. Kiyosaki with Sharon L. Lechter, C.P.A.

The Authors of *Rich Dad Poor Dad*

In association with

momentum media
a division of VideoPlus L.P.

Video *Plus*

This publication is designed to provide general information regarding the subject matter covered. However, laws and practices often vary from state to state and are subject to change. Because each factual situation is different, specific advice should be tailored to the particular circumstances. For this reason, the reader is advised to consult with his or her own advisor regarding that individual's specific situation.

The author has taken reasonable precautions in the preparation of this book and believes the facts presented in the book are accurate as of the date it was written. However, neither the author nor the publisher assume any responsibility for any errors or omissions. The author and publisher specifically disclaim any liability resulting from the use or application of the information contained in this book, and the information is not intended to serve as legal, financial or other professional advice related to individual situations.

Although based on a true story, certain events in the book have been fictionalized for educational content and impact.

Published by TechPress, Inc. in association with CASHFLOW Technologies, Inc. and Momentum Media, a division of VideoPlus, L.P.

CASHFLOW Technologies, Inc.
4330 N. Civic Center Plaza, Suite 101
Scottsdale, Arizona 85251
U.S.A.
800.308.3585
www.richdad.com

CASHFLOW, Rich Dad, Rich Dad's Advisors, Rich Dad's Seminars, EBSI and B-I Triangle are registered trademarks of CASHFLOW Technologies, Inc.

momentum media
a division of VideoPlus, L.P.

Video Plus
200 Swisher Road
Lake Dallas, Texas 75065
U.S.A.
800.752.2030
Tel: 940.497.9700
www.VideoPlus.com

VideoPlus is a registered trademark of VideoPlus, L.P.

Printed in the United States of America

Designed by Momentum Media, a division of VideoPlus, L.P.,
based on the original design by Imagesupport.com, llc

Dedication

We dedicate this book, *The Business School For People Who Like Helping People,* to the millions of individuals, couples and families who have begun their journey starting and building their own businesses through network marketing. As we have dedicated our lives to educating people about how to attain financial freedom, it has been immensely gratifying to associate with an industry that is dedicated to helping people start and build their own businesses. Every day you are educating and sharing your business opportunity with family, friends, neighbors and work associates as well as complete strangers. For this, we honor and thank you. You are seeing firsthand and experiencing the benefits and freedoms of what it is like to have your own business. As our bestselling books *Rich Dad Poor Dad* and *Rich Dad's CASHFLOW Quadrant* explain, once one learns the truths about how money works and the important keys to creating wealth, it is easy to see that having a network marketing business can be "the perfect business" for many people.

Acknowledgements

We were humbled with the tremendous reception the first edition of this book received when it was released in 2001. This pales in comparison, however, to the acceptance the network marketing industry has given our work since the mid-1990s. As a believer in the Rich Dad message, we wish to thank you, your upline, your downline, your crossline and the company with whom you are associated. We are on a mutual quest to help people take control of their financial lives. Keep learning and teaching. We thank you!

Contents

Introduction	*Why Do I Recommend Network Marketing As A Business?*	1
Chapter 1	*What Makes The Rich Rich?*	3
Chapter 2	*There Is More Than One Way To Become Rich*	11
Chapter 3	*Value #1: True Equal Opportunity*	23
Chapter 4	*Value #2: Life-Changing Business Education*	29
Chapter 5	*Value #3: Friends Who Will Pull You Up, Not Push You Down*	41
Chapter 6	*Value #4: What Is The Value Of A Network?*	55
Chapter 7	*Value #5: Developing Your Most Important Business Skill*	61
Chapter 8	*Value #6: Leadership*	75
Chapter 9	*Value #7: Not Working For Money*	85
Chapter 10	*Value #8: Living Your Dreams*	103
Appendices	*Value #9: Marriage And Business*	109
	Value #10: The Family Business	113
	Value #11: How You Can Use The Same Tax Advantages The Rich Use	117
Selected Quotes		121
About The Authors		125
Rich Dad's Resources		129

Why Do I Recommend Network Marketing As A Business?

The following is an example of a type of letter I often receive:

Dear Mr. Kiyosaki,

Hello, hope you are doing well.

My name is Susan and I am writing in regards to my husband, Alan. He has read all your books and has such potential to be a great entrepreneur and businessman. I told him I was going to write you and ask your advice on something. Now personally, I have never read one of your books so I do not know your standing on such topics, but my husband is putting a lot of time into a company called [company name deleted]. They are a pyramid-scheme company that sells vitamins and other health-related products. The person on the top gets you to sell for him, and down the chain it goes. It would not bother me so if I did not feel it was such a waste of his time. Of all his effort to build up someone else's name and company, someone else in the end is going to reap the benefits of his hard work. They sell him on the idea that he is starting his own business, but I do not see his name on the company. How can it be his business if his name is not on the vitamins? On top of that, he's been working at it part-time for over a year and he still has not made much money.

I guess the bottom line is that I think it is a waste of his valuable time, and I would like to see him investing in himself and his own name rather than someone else's. Rather than building a network marketing business, I think he should just start his own company. I also believe the people he is selling for are just using him. Knowing that he has read your books and greatly values your opinion as a businessman, maybe he will listen to your thoughts on this subject because he won't listen to mine. Who knows, maybe I'm wrong. That would be a good thing, as it would put my mind at ease to know.

If you do respond to this letter, I thank you in advance for your time.

Sincerely,

Susan M.

My Response

As some of you may know, my office is swamped with mail. Unfortunately, I do not have the time to respond to every piece of communication I receive.

I start the book with this letter because Susan's concerns and questions are the same ones I often hear from others. They are valid questions and concerns. In addition, I was impressed with her frankness and her willingness to keep an open mind. In today's rapidly changing world, having an open mind is vitally important.

One of the main reasons I decided to write this book is to address such questions and concerns. Many people want to know why I recommend a network marketing business, especially since I am not affiliated with any one company, nor did I make my money with a network marketing business. Therefore, I wrote this book to express my answer once and for all. As you can see from the number of pages in this book, my answer to the above letter is not a simple right or wrong answer.

Before closing, I do not believe a network marketing business is for everyone. It is my hope that by reading this book, you may better know if a network marketing business is right or wrong for you. If you already have a network marketing business, I believe you will find that this book will reaffirm what you already know … and feel. If you are thinking about starting a network marketing business, I believe you will find out about some of the hidden opportunities and values a network marketing business can offer you— values that many people often fail to see. In other words, there is far more to a network marketing business than just the chance to make some extra money.

I thank you in advance for reading this book and for keeping an open mind.

Sincerely,

Robert T. Kiyosaki

CHAPTER 1

What Makes The Rich Rich?

One day after school, I was working in my rich dad's office. I was about 15 years of age at the time and was very frustrated in school. I wanted to learn to be rich, but instead of studying subjects such as "Money 101" or "How To Become a Millionaire 202," I found myself dissecting frogs in science class and wondering how this dead frog would make me rich. Feeling frustrated with school, I asked my rich dad, "Why don't they teach us about money in school?"

Rich dad smiled, looked up from his paper work and said, "I don't know. I've wondered that myself." He paused for a while and then asked, "Why do you ask?"

"Well," I said slowly, "I'm bored in school. I don't see any relevance between what we are required to study in school and the real world. I just want to learn to be rich. So how is a dead frog going to help me buy a new car? If the teacher would tell me how a dead frog can make me rich, I would dissect thousands of them."

Rich dad laughed aloud and asked, "What do they tell you when you ask them about the relationship between dead frogs and money?"

"All my teachers say the same thing," I replied. "They say the same thing no matter how many times I ask them how school is relevant to the real world."

"And what do they say?"

"They say, 'You need to get good grades so you can find a safe secure job,'" I replied.

"Well that is what most people want," said rich dad. "Most people go to school to find a job and some kind of financial security."

"But I don't want to do that. I don't want to be an employee working for someone else. I don't want to spend my life having someone else tell me how much money I can earn or when I can go to work or take a vacation. I want to be free. I want to be rich. That is why I don't want a job."

For those of you who may not have read *Rich Dad Poor Dad,* my rich dad was my best friend's father. Although he was a man who started with nothing and did not have a formal education, he ultimately became one of the wealthiest men in the State of Hawaii. My poor dad, my real dad, was a highly educated man, a highly paid government official, but no matter how much money he made, he was broke at the end of every month and ultimately died broke with little to show for a life of hard work.

One of the reasons I began studying with my rich dad after school and on weekends was because I knew that I was not receiving the education I wanted in school. I knew school did not have the answers I was searching for because my real dad, my poor dad, was the head of education for the State of Hawaii. I knew that my real dad, the head teacher, did not know much about money. Therefore, I knew the school system could not teach me what I wanted to know. At the age of 15, I wanted to know how to be rich rather than how to be an employee who works for the rich.

After seeing my mom and dad constantly fight over not having enough money, I began to look for an adult who could teach me about money. That is how I came to study with my rich dad. I studied with him from the age of nine until I was 38 years of age. I was looking for the education. For me, it was my "Business School"—the business school for real life. Because of my rich dad's training, I was able to retire at the age of 47, financially free for the rest of my life. If I had followed my poor dad's advice—the advice of being a good employee until I was 65 years old—I would still be working today, worried about my job security and worried about my pension plan filled with mutual funds that keep going down in value. The difference between my rich dad's advice and my poor dad's advice was simple. My poor dad always said, "Go to school and get good grades so you can find a safe, secure job with benefits." My rich dad's advice was, "If you want to be rich, you need to be a business owner and an investor." My problem was that school did not teach me to own businesses or to be an investor.

> **"If you want to be rich, you need to be a business owner and an investor."**

Why Thomas Edison Was Rich And Famous

"So what did you study in school today?" asked rich dad.

Thinking about my day for a while, I finally replied: "We have been studying the life of Thomas Edison."

"That's an important person to study," said rich dad. "So, did you discuss how he became rich and famous?"

"No," I replied. "We only discussed his inventions, like the light bulb."

Rich dad smiled and said, "Well, I hate to contradict your teacher, but Thomas Edison did not invent the light bulb…but he did perfect it." Rich dad explained that Thomas Edison was one of his heroes and he had studied his life.

"So, why is he credited with inventing it?" I asked.

"There were other light bulbs invented before his light bulb, but the problem was they were not practical. The early bulbs did not burn long enough. Also, the other inventors could not explain how the light bulb could have any commercial value."

"Commercial value?" I asked in a puzzled tone.

"In other words, the other inventors did not know how to make money from their invention…and Thomas Edison did," added rich dad.

"So, he invented the first *useful* light bulb and he also knew how to turn the bulb into a business," I stated.

Rich dad nodded his head, "And it was his business sense that made so many of his inventions so useful to millions of people. Thomas Edison was more than an inventor. He was the founder of General Electric and many other major companies. Did your teachers explain that to you?"

"No," I replied. "I wish they would have. I would have been more interested in the subject. Instead, I was bored and wondering how Thomas Edison was relevant to real life. If they have told me how he became so rich, I would have been much more interested and listened more closely."

Rich dad laughed and told me how Thomas Edison the inventor also became a multi-millionaire and founder of a billion-dollar corporation. Rich dad went on to say that Edison dropped out of school because his teachers thought he was not smart enough to succeed in school. He then took a job selling candies and magazines on the railroads as a young boy. There, he developed his sales skills. Soon, he began to print his own newspaper in the back of the train and then hired a team of boys to sell not only his candies, but also his newspaper. While still a boy, he went from employee to business owner, employing a dozen other boys, in about a year.

"So that is how Thomas Edison began his business career?" I asked.

Rich dad nodded his head and smiled.

"Why didn't the teachers tell me that?" I asked. "I would have loved to have heard that story."

"There is more," said rich dad as he continued with Edison's story. Edison soon grew bored of his business on the train and began learning how to send and receive Morse code so he could get a job as a telegraph operator. Soon, Edison was one of the best telegraph operators around and he traveled from city to city using his telegraph operator skills. "It was what he learned from being a young entrepreneur and a telegraph operator that gave him the edge as a businessperson and an inventor of the light bulb."

"How did being a telegraph operator help him become a better businessman?" I asked, now confused. "What does this story have to do with me becoming rich?"

"Give me time to explain," said rich dad. "You see, Thomas Edison was more than just an inventor. As a young boy, he became a business owner. That is why he became very rich and famous. Rather than going to school, he gained the business skills required for success in the real world. You asked me why the rich get rich, didn't you?"

"Yes," I replied, nodding and feeling a little embarrassed for interrupting my rich dad.

"What made him famous relative to the light bulb was his past experience as a businessperson and a telegraph operator," rich dad said. "Being a telegraph operator, he knew that what made the inventor of the telegraph so successful was because it was a business system—a system of lines, poles, skilled people, and relay stations. As a young man, Thomas Edison understood the power of a system."

I jumped in, "You mean because he was a businessperson, he realized how important the system was. The system was more important than the invention."

Rich dad nodded. "You see, most people go to school to learn to be an employee of a system; they fail to see the big picture. Most only see the value of their job because that is all they are trained to see. So, they see the trees and not the forest."

"So, most people work for the system rather than own the system," I added.

Nodding in agreement, rich dad said, "All they see is the invention or product, but not the system. Most people fail to see what really makes the rich rich."

"So, how does this apply to Thomas Edison and the electric light bulb?" I asked.

"What made the light bulb powerful was not the light bulb, but the system of electrical lines and relay stations that powered the light bulb," said rich dad. "What made Thomas Edison rich and famous was that he could see the big picture while other people only saw the light bulb."

"And he could see the big picture because of his business experience on the train and his experience as a telegraph operator," I replied.

Rich dad nodded. "Another word for system is 'network.' If you really want to learn how to be rich, you must begin to know and understand the power found in *networks*. The richest people in the world build networks.

Everyone else is trained to look for work."

"The richest people in the world build networks. Everyone else is trained to look for work."

"Without the electrical network, the light bulb would have very little value to people," I said.

"You're getting the idea," smiled rich dad. "So what makes the rich rich is that they build and own the system…the network. Owning the network makes them rich."

"A network? So if I want to become rich, I need to learn how to build a business network?" I queried.

"You're getting the idea," rich dad said, "There is more than one way to become rich, but the ultra-rich have always built networks. Just look at how John D. Rockefeller became one of the wealthiest men in the world. He did more than just drill for oil. John D. Rockefeller became one of the richest men in the world because he built a network of gas stations, delivery trucks, ships and pipelines. He became so rich and powerful because of his network that the U.S. government forced him to break up his network, calling it a monopoly."

"And, Alexander Graham Bell invented the telephone, which eventually became a telephone network called AT&T," I added.

Rich dad nodded. "And later came radio networks and then television networks. Every time a new invention came along, the people who got rich were the people who built and owned the network that supported the new invention. Many high-paid stars and sports athletes are rich simply because radio and television networks make them rich and famous."

"So why doesn't our school system teach us to build networks?" I asked.

Rich dad shrugged his shoulders. "I don't know," he replied. "I think because most people are just happy to find a job working as an employee of a large network…a network that makes the rich richer. I did not want to work for the rich. That is why I built my own network. I did not make as much money early in my life, because it takes time to build a network. For five years, I made much less than my peers did. However, after 10 years, I was far richer than most of my classmates, even the ones who went on to become doctors and lawyers. Today, I earn far more than they could ever dream of earning. A well designed and managed business network will exponentially earn far more than a hard-working individual can."

Rich dad explained that history is filled with stories of rich and famous people who built networks. When trains were invented, many people became rich. The same is true for airplanes, ships, cars and retail stores like Wal-Mart,

Gap and Radio Shack. In today's world, the power of super computers and the power of PC's allow many individuals the power to build great wealth if they would work to build their own networks. This book and my company, richdad.com, are dedicated to those who want to build their own business networks.

Today we have Bill Gates, the richest man in the world, who became rich plugging an operating system into IBM's network. The Beatles became famous worldwide due to the power of the radio, television and record store networks. Sport stars earn millions of dollars due to the power of television and radio networks. The Internet, which is the latest in worldwide networks, has made many people millionaires and even a few people billionaires. My writing skills have earned millions of dollars not because I am a great writer but because my business partners with the Time Warner network. We at richdad.com work cooperatively with Time Warner Books and AOL on the Internet. They are great companies and great people to work with. Richdad.com is also networking with other companies throughout the world, in countries such as Japan, China, Australia, the UK, Europe, Africa, South America, Canada, India, Singapore, Malaysia, Indonesia, Mexico, Philippines and Taiwan. As rich dad said, "The rich build networks and everyone else looks for work."

Why The Rich Get Richer

Most of us have heard the saying, "Birds of a feather flock together." Well, that saying holds true not only for birds, but also for rich people, poor people and middle-class people. In other words, the rich network with the rich; the poor network with other poor people; and the middle class hangs out with the middle class. Rich dad often said, "If you want to become rich, you need to network with those who are rich or who can help you become rich." He also said, "Many people spend their lives hanging out and networking with people who hold them back financially." One idea this book wants to pass on is that a networking marketing business is a business with people who are there to help you become richer. One question you may want to ask yourself is this: "Is the company I work for and are the people with whom I spend time dedicated to me becoming rich? Or, are the people and company more interested in me continuing on as a hard worker?"

By the age of 15, I knew that one way for me to become rich and financially free was to learn how to network with people who could help me become rich and financially free. To me, that made perfect sense. Yet, to many of my high school classmates, what made sense was to get good grades and get a safe, secure job. At the age of 15, I decided that I would seek the friendship of friends who were interested in me becoming a rich person rather than becoming a loyal employee working for the rich. When I look back upon my life, the decision I made at the age of 15 was a life-changing decision. It was not an easy decision because at 15, I had to be very careful with whom I spent my time and which teachers to whom I would listen. For those of you considering building your own business, this idea—the idea of being aware of whom you spend your time with and who your teachers are—is a very important consideration. As a young boy in high school, I began choosing my friends and teachers very carefully, because your family, friends and teachers are a very, very, very important element of your network.

A Business School For The People

Personally, I am thrilled to write this book in support of the network marketing industry. Many companies in this industry are offering millions of people the same business education my rich dad taught me: the opportunity to build your own network rather than spend your life working for a network.

Teaching people to understand the power of building their own business, their own network, is not an easy task. The reason is that most people have been taught to be loyal, hard-working employees rather than to be business owners who build their own networks.

After I returned from Vietnam, where I was a U.S. Marine Corps officer and helicopter pilot, I considered going back to school to get my M.B.A. degree. My rich dad talked me out of it. He said, "If you get a M.B.A. from a traditional school, you are still trained to be an employee of the rich. If you want to be rich, rather than a highly paid employee of the rich, you need to go to a business school that teaches you to be an entrepreneur. That is the type of business school I have put you through." Rich dad also said, "The problem with most business schools is that they take the smartest kids and train them to be business executives for the rich, rather than executives for the employees." If you followed the news on Enron and WorldCom, the highly educated executives were accused of thinking only of themselves, and not the employees or investors who had entrusted their lives and money with them. Many highly educated and highly paid executives were telling their employees to buy more of the company stock while the executives were selling theirs. Although WorldCom and Enron are extreme cases, that type of selfish behavior goes on every day in the corporate world and in the stock market.

A big reason I support the network marketing industry is that many companies in the industry are really *business schools for the people* rather than business schools that take smart kids and train them to be employees of the rich. Many network marketing companies teach values not found in traditional business schools...values such as the best way to become rich is to teach yourself and other people to become business owners...rather than teach them to be loyal employees working for the rich.

Other Ways Of Getting Rich

Many people have acquired great wealth building a network marketing business. In fact, some of my richest friends have created their fortune building a network marketing business. Yet, to be fair, there are other ways a person can acquire great wealth. Therefore, in the next chapter, this book will go into other ways people have become rich and, more importantly, financially free...free from the drudgery of earning a living, clinging to job security, and living paycheck to paycheck. After reading the next chapter, you may have a better idea of whether building a network marketing business is the best way for you to create your own personal fortune...and as a vehicle to pursue your dreams and passions.

CHAPTER 2

There Is More Than One Way To Become Rich

"Can you teach me to be rich?" I asked my teacher.

"No," my biology teacher replied. "My job is to help you graduate so you can find a good job."

"But what if I don't want a job? What if I want to be rich?" I asked.

"Why do you want to be rich?" asked my teacher.

"Because I want to be free. I want to have the money and time to do what I want to do. I don't want to be an employee for most of my life. I don't want my life's dreams to be dictated by the size of my paycheck."

"That's nonsense. You're dreaming about the life of the idle rich and you can't be rich if you don't have good grades and a high-paying job," said the teacher. "Now get back to your frog."

In my other books and educational programs, I often refer to the three different types of education that are required if we want to be financially successful in life: scholastic, professional and financial education.

Scholastic Education

This education teaches us to read, write and do math. It is a very important education, especially in today's world. Personally, I did not do well with this level of education. I was a "C" student most of my life simply because I was not interested in what I was being taught. I am a very slow reader, and I do not write well. Although a slow reader, I do read a lot; I just read very slowly, and I often have to read a book two or three times before I understand what I am reading.

I am also a poor writer, though I continue to write.

As a side note, although a poor writer, I have been fortunate to have seven books on *The New York Times, The Wall Street Journal* and *BusinessWeek* best-seller lists. As I state in *Rich Dad Poor Dad,* I am not a best-writing author, I am a best-selling author. My rich dad's sales training did pay off even though it did not pay off in school when it came to my grades.

Professional Education

This education teaches you how to work for money. During my youth, the smart kids went on to become doctors, lawyers and accountants. Other professional schools teach people to become medical assistants, plumbers, builders, electricians and automobile mechanics. If you look in the yellow pages of your phone book under education or schools, you will find those pages filled with schools that teach people professions that help them become more employable.

Personally, since I did not do well at the first level of education—the scholastic level—becoming a doctor, lawyer or accountant was not encouraged for me. Instead, I attended school in New York where I became a ship's officer, sailing ships such as tankers for Standard Oil and passenger liners like the ship on the television program, *The Love Boat.* After graduation, because the Vietnam War was on, instead of taking a job in the shipping industry, I went to Pensacola, Florida where I attended the U.S. Navy Flight School and became a pilot, flying for the Marine Corps in Vietnam. Both my dads said it was a son's duty to fight for his country, so both my brother and I volunteered to go to Vietnam. By the time I was 23, I had two professions: one as a ship's officer and the other as a pilot, but I never really used either of them to make money.

On a side note, I think it ironic today that the skill I am most known for is writing...a subject I failed twice in high school.

Financial Education

This is the education where you learn to have *money work for you* rather than to have *you work for money.* This third level of education is not taught in most of our schools.

My poor dad thought that a good scholastic and professional education was all a person needed to be successful in the real world. My rich dad said, "If you have a poor financial education, you will always work for the rich." Richdad.com has done its best to create products that teach the same financial education my rich dad taught me. We have products such as the board games *CASHFLOW 101, 202* and *CASHFLOW for Kids,* which teach in a *fun way* the same financial education and financial mindset my rich dad taught me.

> **"Learn to have *money work for you* rather than to have *you work for money*."**

A Financial Disaster

In my opinion, the United States and many Western nations have a financial disaster coming...a financial disaster caused by our educational systems' failure to adequately provide a realistic financial education program for students. As most of us unfortunately know, we did not receive much financial education in school, and, in my opinion, knowing how to manage and invest money is a very important life skill.

Recently, we have seen millions of people lose trillions of dollars in the stock market. In the near future, I predict a financial disaster because millions of people born after 1950 will not have enough money for retirement. More important than money for retirement is money for medical care. I often hear financial advisors saying, "Your living expenses go down after you retire." What those financial advisors often fail to tell you is that after you retire what goes up are your medical expenses, even if your living expenses go down.

My poor dad believed that the government should take care of anyone who did not have money. While in my heart I agree with him, my financial mind wonders how our government can afford to provide for the millions of people who will soon need financial support for living and medical expenses. By the year 2010, the first of 83 million baby boomers will begin to retire. My question is how many of them have enough money to survive once their working days are over? And if millions will need billions of dollars to survive, are the young people of the world willing to pay for the living expenses of the old people?

In my opinion, it is imperative that our school systems begin teaching financial education as soon as possible. Learning how to manage and invest money is certainly as important as learning how to dissect a frog.

A Personal Comment

My wife and I were able to retire early in life without a job, without government assistance, and without any stocks or mutual funds. Why did we not have stocks or mutual funds? The reason is, in our opinion, they are very risky investments. In my opinion, mutual funds are some of the riskiest of all investments; yet, they are a good investment if you do not have any formal financial education and experience.

If you have follow the financial news, you may have noticed that before the stock market crash, which started in March of 2000, the financial advisors were saying, "Invest for the long-term, buy and hold, and diversify." Now that the market has crashed, they are advising, "Invest for the long-term, buy and hold, and diversify." Do you notice anything different?

So, if you *do not* have a good financial education, then you may want to do as most financial advisors advise, which is to save money, buy mutual funds, invest for the long-term and diversify. If you have a strong financial education, then you may not have to follow such risky advice. Instead, you can do what my rich dad advised me to do, which is to first build a business. He said, "Building your own business is the best way to become rich." Rich dad also said, "After you have built your business, and you have strong cash flow, then you can begin investing in other assets."

> **"Building your own business is the best way to become rich. After you have built your business, and you have strong cash flow, then you can begin investing in other assets."**

The Other Ways To Become Rich

Rich dad said, "Because so many people do not have an adequate financial education, they come up with many interesting ways to become rich other than building a business network. For example, millions of people try to become rich playing the lottery or working hard and saving money. And some people actually do become rich using these different methods." He also said, "If you want to become rich, you need to find the way to become rich that best works for you." The following are some of the other ways people become rich.

1. You can become rich by marrying someone for his or her money. This is a very popular way of becoming rich. Yet, rich dad would say, "You *know* what kind of person marries for money."

2. You can become rich by being a crook. Rich dad said, "The trouble with being a crook is that you have to associate with other crooks. Much of business is based on trust. How can you have much trust when your partners are crooks?" He also said, "If you are honest and make an honest mistake in business, most people understand and give you a second chance. In addition, if you learn from your honest mistakes, you will grow into a better businessperson. But if you are a crook and you make a mistake, then you either go to jail or your partners will punish you in their own efficient ways."

3. You can become rich by being greedy. My rich dad said, "The world is filled with people who became rich by being greedy. Greedy rich people are the most despised of all the different types of rich people."

After the stock market crash of 2000, the world feasted on stories of companies that distorted their financial records, CEOs who lied to investors, insiders who sold stock illegally, and corporate officers who told their workers to buy shares while they were selling theirs. For months, the news was filled with stories about the leaders of Enron, WorldCom, Arthur Andersen and Wall Street analysts who were lying, cheating and stealing. In other words, some of these rich greedy people were so greedy they broke laws and turned into crooks. The first few years of the 21st century revealed some of the worst examples of greed, corruption and lack of moral guidance, proving that not all crooks deal in drugs, wear masks and rob banks.

4. You can become rich by being cheap. Rich dad said, "Trying to become rich by being cheap is the *most* popular way people attempt to become rich. People who try to become rich by being cheap are people who often try to live below their means rather than finding ways to expand their means." He also said, "The problem with becoming rich by being cheap is that in the end you're still cheap." We have all heard stories of people who spent their lives hoarding money, pinching pennies, and shopping at sales just to acquire masses of money. Yet, even though they have a lot of money, they live life as poorly as someone who is truly poor. To my rich dad, having a lot of money yet living like a poor person made very little sense.

Rich dad had a friend who lived cheaply all his life, saving his money, never spending on anything except for the bare necessities. The sad thing was that his three grown children could not wait for him to die so they could get their hands on all his money. After he passed away, his three children made up for all the years of living cheap and spent all his money in less than three years. After all the money was gone, the kids were just as poor as their dad was, even though he once had lots of money. To my rich dad, people who hoard money yet live poorly are people who worship money, making money their master rather than learn to become a master of money.

5. You can become rich via hard work. The problem rich dad had with hard work was that he noticed that hard-working people often had a hard time enjoying their money and their life. In other words, hard work was all they knew. They did not know how to have a good time.

Working Hard For A Bad Income

Rich dad also taught his son and me that many people work hard for the wrong kind of income. He said, "People who physically work hard for money often work hard for the wrong kind of income. Income that is physically worked for is the highest taxed of all income. People who work for the wrong income often work harder and harder only to be taxed more and more." In my rich dad's mind, to work for income that is taxed more and more was not financially intelligent. Most people who have a job work for the highest taxed of all income. In addition, the people who are paid the least often pay the highest percentage in taxes.

When I was a boy, my rich dad taught me that there is more than one kind of income. He said, "There is good income and bad income." In this book, you will find out what kind of income to work hard for…which is income that is taxed less and less even though you earn more and more.

Rich dad also pointed out to his son and me that many people work very hard all their lives but had little to show for their hard work at the end of their lives. In this book, you will find out how you may have to work hard for a few years but eventually be free to choose never to work again…if that is what you choose to do.

6. You can become rich by being exceptionally smart, talented, attractive or gifted. Tiger Woods is an example of an exceptionally gifted golfer—a golfer who spent years developing his gift. Yet being gifted, smart or talented is still no guarantee of becoming rich. Rich dad would say, "The world is filled with gifted people who never become rich. Just go to Hollywood and you find many beautiful, handsome and talented actors who earn less than most people." Statistics also show that 65 percent of all professional athletes are broke five years after their high-paying professional careers are over. In the world of money, it takes more than God-given brains, talent or good looks to become rich.

7. You can become rich by being lucky. Trying to become rich by being lucky is almost as popular as trying to become rich by being cheap. As most of us know, millions of people bet billions, maybe trillions, of dollars on the lottery, the race tracks, casinos and on sporting events, all hoping to strike it rich by being lucky. Moreover, as we all know, for every lucky person there are thousands, maybe millions, of unlucky people. Again, studies have shown that most lottery winners are broke five years after winning more money than they could have earned in five lifetimes. Therefore, even being lucky once or twice does not mean you hold on to your wealth.

8. You can become rich by inheriting money. By the time we are in our twenties, we should know if we are going to inherit anything. If you know you are not going to inherit anything, then obviously you need to find some other way to become rich.

9. You can become rich by investing. One of the most common complaints I have is that it takes money to invest. In addition, in most cases that is true. There is another problem with investing. You can lose everything you invest if you are not financially educated and trained to be an investor. As many of us have seen, the stock market is risky and volatile, which means one day you make money and the next day it could be all gone. With real estate, although you can use your banker's money to invest, it still takes some money and education to accumulate great wealth. In this book, you will find out how to acquire the money to invest. More importantly, you will learn how to become an investor before you risk your money.

10. You can become rich by building a business. Building a business is the way most of the rich became very rich. Bill Gates built Microsoft; Michael Dell created Dell Computers in his dormitory room. The problem is that building a business from scratch remains the riskiest of all the ways to become rich. Even purchasing a franchise, which is less risky, can be very expensive. Prices to purchase well-known franchises may range from $100,000 to $1.5 million just for the rights to the franchise. On top of the initial fee, there are monthly payments to the headquarters for training, advertising and support. In addition, even all this support is still no guarantee of great wealth. Many times a person must continue to pay money to the franchisor or headquarters, even when his or her personal franchise is losing money. Although buying a franchise is less risky than starting your own business from nothing, statistics show that 1/3 of all franchises eventually go broke.

The Difference Between Big Business Owners And Small Business Owners

Before moving on to the eleventh way of becoming rich, I want to discuss the difference between a small-business owner and a big-business owner. The difference is that big-business people build networks. The world is filled with small-business owners who own restaurants. The difference between a single-restaurant owner and Ray Kroc, who founded McDonalds, is that McDonalds is a network of hamburger restaurants known as a franchise network. Another example, in contrast, is a small-business owner who owns a television repair shop as compared to Ted Turner, who built CNN, which stands for Cable News Network. Again, notice the word *network*. The point is that the difference between a small-business owner and a big-business owner is simply the size of their network. While many small-business owners own businesses, very few business owners build networks. Simply put, building a business network is how the richest people in the world became rich.

The Eleventh Way To Become Rich

11. You can build a network marketing business. The reason I put a network marketing business as the eleventh way of becoming rich is that it is a very new and revolutionary way to aquire great wealth. If you will quickly glance over the first 10 ways of becoming rich, you may notice that the focus is a self-centered focus on who becomes rich. In other words, it might be seen as a greedy focus. For example, someone who tries to become rich by being cheap is primarily focused on themselves and maybe a few family and friends becoming rich. Someone who marries for money is definitely focused on the money for himself or herself. Even a big business is focused on only a few selected people becoming rich. When franchises came out they made it possible for more people to become business owners and share in the wealth, but in most cases, franchises are reserved for only those with the money to buy the franchise, and, as I stated earlier, a McDonalds franchise today costs over $1 million to get in. Therefore, I am not saying these people are bad or greedy people; I am simply saying that in most cases, the focus is not on a lot of people becoming rich. The focus is on the individual becoming rich.

> **"A network marketing business is a new and revolutionary way to achieve wealth."**

The reason I put network marketing as an eleventh way of becoming rich all by itself is because it is a revolutionary new way of sharing the wealth with anyone who truly wants to acquire great wealth. A network marketing system is set up to make it possible for anyone to share in the wealth. A network marketing system—a system I often call a *personal franchise* or an *invisible big business network*—is, in my opinion, a very democratic way of wealth creation. The system is open to anyone who has drive, determination and perseverance. The system does not really care what college you went to, if you went to one, how much money you make today, what race or sex you are, how good-looking you are, who your parents are, or how popular you are. Most network marketing companies care primarily about how much you are willing to learn, to change and to grow, and whether you have the guts to stick it out through thick and thin while you learn to be a business owner.

> **"A network marketing system—a system I often call a personal franchise—is a very democratic way of wealth creation. "**

Recently, I listened to an audio recording of a very famous and rich investor, delivering a speech to a famous business school. I do not mention the school's name or his name because what I am about to say is not very flattering. He said, "I am not interested in teaching people to invest. I am not interested in helping poor people get ahead in life. All I want to do is spend time with intelligent people like you, here at (the famous business school.)"

While I personally do not agree with what he said, I still commend him for his honesty. As a person who spent much of my life growing up with the rich friends of my rich dad, I often heard such comments, but they were said discreetly and quietly. In public, they would attend charity events and donate money to popular causes, but many of them did that only to appear socially acceptable. In their private meetings, I often heard their real thoughts— thoughts that were of similar context to the famous investor speaking at the famous business school.

Obviously, not all rich people share that attitude. Nonetheless, I am constantly amazed at how many rich and successful people are rich and successful because they are greedy and have very little interest in helping those less fortunate. Again, I will state that not all rich people share this attitude, but the percentage is significant from my experience.

A primary reason I support the network marketing industry is that their systems are fairer than previous systems of acquiring wealth. Henry Ford, one of the world's greatest businesspersons, became rich by fulfilling the mission statement of his company, the Ford Motor Company. Ford's mission statement was, "Democratize the automobile." The reason that mission statement was so revolutionary was because at the turn of the century, automobiles were only available to the rich. Henry Ford's idea was to make the automobile affordable for everyone, which is what "Democratize the automobile" means. Interestingly enough, Henry Ford was an employee of Thomas Edison, and in his spare time, Henry designed his first automobile. In 1903, the Ford Motor Company was born. By slashing production costs and adapting the assembly line to mass-produce standardized inexpensive cars, Ford became the largest automobile producer in the world. Not only did he make his car affordable; he paid the highest wages in the industry as well as offering profit sharing plans for his workers, redistributing over $30 million annually to them...and $30 million was worth a lot more in the early 1900s than it is today.

In other words, Henry Ford was a man who became rich because he cared not only for his customers, but because he cared for his workers. He was a generous man rather than a greedy man. Henry Ford also came under much criticism and personal attack by the so-called intellectual society. Henry Ford was not well educated and, like Thomas Edison, was often ridiculed because of his lack of formal education.

One of my favorite stories of Henry Ford was when he was asked to submit to a test by so-called smart people from the world of academics. On the appointed day, a group of smart people came in to give him an oral test. They wanted to prove he was ignorant.

The test began by one scholar asking him a question such as, "What is the tensile strength of the rolled steel you use." Ford, not knowing the answer, simply reached for one of the many phones on his desk and called his vice president who knew the answer. The vice president came in, and Ford asked him the question. The vice president gave him the answer the panel wanted. The next smart person then asked another question and again Ford, not knowing the answer, called someone else from his staff who knew the answer. This process went on until finally one of the smart people on the panel shouted, "See, this proves you are ignorant. You don't know the answers to any of the questions we ask you."

Henry Ford reportedly replied, "I don't know the answers because I do not need to clutter my head with the answers you seek. I hire smart young people from your schools who have memorized the answers you expect me to have memorized. My job is to not to memorize information that you think is intelligence. My job is to keep my head clear of such clutter and trivial facts so that I can think." At that point, he asked the smart people from the world of academics to leave.

For years, I have committed to memory what I believe is one of Henry Ford's most important sayings: "Thinking is the hardest work there is. That is why so few people engage in it."

> **"Thinking is the hardest work there is. That is why so few people engage in it."**

Wealth For Everyone

In my opinion, this new form of business, the network marketing business, is a revolution simply because for the first time in history it is now possible for anyone and everyone to share in the wealth that, until now, has been reserved only for the chosen few or the lucky. I am aware that there has been some controversy over this new form of business and it's had its share of greedy and sometimes crooked people trying to make a quick buck. Yet, if you step back and look at this new form of business, it is a very socially responsible system of sharing the wealth. A network marketing business is not a good business for greedy people. By design, it is the perfect business for people who like helping other people. Saying it another way, the only way a network marketing business works is by helping someone else become rich as you become rich. To me, that is revolutionary, just as revolutionary as Thomas Edison and Henry Ford were in their days.

Before closing, I know that most people are generous. I am also not condemning greed, since a little greed and personal self-interest is always healthy. It is when greed or personal gain becomes excessive that most of us protest or shake our heads in disgust. Since most people are generous and want to help their fellow human beings, this new form of networking business systems gives more people the power to help many more people. While this business is not for everyone, if you are a person who truly wants to help as many people as possible achieve their financial goals and dreams, then the network marketing business is worthy of your time to consider.

In Summary

Today there are many ways for a person to become rich. The best way to become rich is to find the way that works best for you. If you are a person who loves helping other people, I believe this new form of business system— network marketing—is for you. That is why I have titled this book *The Business School For People Who Like Helping Other People*. If helping other people is not your cup of tea, then there are at least 10 other methods to choose from.

In the following chapters, I will be discussing the core values I have found in most network marketing companies. In my opinion, these core values are the most important for you to consider in deciding whether or not you will be a part of this industry. Rich dad taught his son and me that core values are far more important than money. He often said, "You can become rich by being cheap and greedy. You can also become rich by being abundant and generous. The method you choose will be the method that most closely matches the core values deep inside of you."

CHAPTER 3

Value#1: True Equal Opportunity

I am often asked, "Since you did not become rich from building a network marketing business, why do you recommend others get into the business?" There are several reasons I recommend the network marketing business, and they are explained in this book.

The Closing Of My Mind

It was sometime during the mid-1970s that a friend invited me to a presentation on a new business opportunity. Being a person who makes it a habit of regularly investigating business and investment opportunities, I agreed to attend the meeting. Although I thought it was strange that the business meeting was at a private home rather than in an office, I went along anyway. That meeting was to be my introduction to the world of network marketing.

I sat there patiently listening to the three-hour presentation. I agreed with most of the points on why someone should start their own business. The part I did not pay much attention to was how the business they were building was so very different from the business I was building. Simply put, I was building my business to make me rich and they were talking about building a business that made many people rich. At that stage of my life, my mind was not open to such radical new ideas. In my mind, a business is supposed to make only the owners rich.

At the end of the evening, the friend asked me what I thought of the business opportunity presented. My reply was, "It was interesting but it's not for me." When my friend asked me why I was not interested I said, "I am already building my own business. Why do I need to build a business with other people? Why should I help them?" I then said, "Besides, I have heard rumors that these network marketing businesses are just pyramid schemes and are illegal." Before my friend could say anything further, I walked off into the night, got into my car, and drove away.

At that stage of my life in the mid-1970s, I was building my first international business. Therefore, I was very busy keeping my daytime job and building this business in my spare time. The business I was building was a manufacturing and marketing business focused on bringing to market the first nylon and Velcro surfer wallets. Soon after my first network marketing meeting, my sports wallet business boomed. My two years of hard work was paying off. Success, fame and fortune seemed to pour down upon my two partners and me. We had reached our goal, which was to become millionaires before we were 30. In the 1970s, $1 million was worth something. My company and my products were written about in such magazines as *Surfer, Runner's World* and *Gentleman's Quarterly.* We were the hot new products in the sporting goods world, and business poured in from all over the world. My first international business was up and running. Therefore, when presented with the business opportunity a network marketing business offered me, my mind was closed and I did not want to hear anymore. It would be years before it would open again...open enough to listen and to begin to change my opinion about the industry. I did not think about the network marketing industry again for 15 years.

A Change Of Mind

Sometime in the early 1990s a friend I respect for his financial wisdom and his business success told me he was in the network marketing business. Bill was already very wealthy from his real estate investments, so it puzzled me why he would have a network marketing business. Now curious, I asked him, "Why are you in this business? You don't need the money, do you?"

Laughing aloud, Bill said, "You know I like making money, but I am not in the business because I need the money. My finances are in great shape."

I knew that Bill had just completed commercial real estate projects worth over $1 billion in the last two years, so I also knew he was doing well. Yet his vague answer made me more curious, so I pressed on, asking him, "So, why do you have a network marketing business?"

Bill thought for a long while and then began speaking in his slow Texas style: "For years, people have asked me for real estate investment tips. They want to know how to become rich by investing in real estate. Many want to know if they can invest with me or how they can find real estate for no money down."

Nodding in agreement I said, "I am asked the same questions."

"The problem is," said Bill continuing on, "most cannot invest with me because they do not have enough money. They do not have the $50,000 or $100,000 needed to get into my level of real estate investments. In addition, the reason many of them want a no-money-down deal is that many of them have absolutely no money at all. Some are two paychecks away from bankruptcy. Therefore, they look for these cheap no-money-down deals that are often very bad deals. You and I know the best real estate deals go to the rich who have money and not to those without money."

Nodding, I said, "I understand. I remember being so poor that no banker or real estate agent would take me seriously. You mean they don't have any money, or if they do have money, they don't have enough money for you to help them. They aren't rich enough for your investments?"

Bill nodded, "And on top of that, if they do have a little money, it is often their life savings. You know I do not recommend investing everything you have. On top of that, if they invest their life savings, they are often so afraid of losing they wind up losing. And you and I know that a person who is afraid of losing often loses."

My conversation with Bill went on for a few more minutes, but I soon had to dash for the airport. I was still not sure why he was in a network marketing business, but my closed mind was beginning to open. I was beginning to want to know more about why someone as rich as he was had a network marketing business. I was beginning to realize that there was something more to the business than just the money.

Over the next few months my dialogue with Bill continued. Slowly I began to understand his reasons for being in the business. His primary reasons were:

1. He wanted to help people. This was his main reason for having this business. Although a very rich man, he was not a greedy or arrogant man.

2. He wanted to help himself. "You have to be rich to invest with me. I realized that if I helped more people become rich, then I would have more investors." Bill continued, "The irony is that the more I helped others become rich building their own business, the more my business grew…and I became richer. Now I have a thriving consumer distribution business, more investors, and more money of my own to invest. Talk about win-win. That is why in the last few years I have begun investing in much larger real estate projects. As you know, it's hard to get really rich investing in small real estate deals. It can be done, but if you don't have much money, all you get are the real estate deals that people with money don't want."

3. He loves learning and teaching. "I love working with people who want to learn." He said to me in one of our later discussions, "It is exhausting working with people who think they know everything. In my world of real estate investing, I work with many of those people. Working with someone who thinks they know all the answers is tough. For me, people who start a network marketing business are looking for new answers and they are ready to learn. I love learning, teaching business, and sharing new ideas with people excited about their ongoing education. As you know, I have a degree in accounting and an M.B.A. in finance. This business gives me a chance to teach others what I know and continue learning along with everyone else. You would be surprised how many very smart, well educated people from different backgrounds are in this business. There are also many people without a formal education who are in this business to gain the education they need to find financial security in a world with less and less job security. We get together and share what we already know from our life's experiences and what we are learning. I love teaching and I love learning, and that is why I love this business. It's a great business and a great real-life business school."

A Newly Opened Mind

So sometime during the early 1990s my mind began to open and my point of view on the network marketing industry began to change. I began to see things that my closed mind could not see. I began to see things that were good and positive about the industry rather than the things that were negative...and there are negatives to the industry. But then again, there is something negative about most things.

After retiring in 1994, financially free at the age of 47, I began my own research into the network marketing industry. Anytime someone invited me to one of his or her presentations, I went along just to listen to what he or she had to say. I did join a few of the network marketing companies if I liked what they said. However, I joined not necessarily to make more money; I joined to take a long hard look at the positives and the negatives of each company. Instead of just closing my mind, I wanted to find my own answers. After looking into several companies, I saw the negatives that most people see at first glance such as the strange people who initially come into the industry and promote their business. It is true that many dreamers, hustlers, con men, losers and get-rich-quick artists are attracted to this type of business. One of the challenges of a network marketing business is that they have an open door policy, which allows almost anyone to join. This open-door policy is the fair and equal opportunity that most socialists cry out for, yet I did not meet many hard-core socialists in these businesses meetings. These businesses are for capitalists or at least for people who hope to become capitalists.

> **"A network marketing business has an open door policy."**

After getting through the masses of wannabes, hustlers and dreamers, I finally began meeting the leaders of some of the companies. The ones I met were some of the most intelligent, kind, ethical, moral, spiritual and professional people I have met in all my years of business. Once I got over my own prejudices and met people I respected and related to, I found the heart of the industry. I could now see what I could not see before. I could now see the good and the bad.

Therefore, this book is written in part to answer the question, "Since you did not become rich from building a network marketing business, why do you recommend that others get into the business?" It is because I did not gain my fortune from building a network marketing business that I can be a bit more objective about the industry. This book describes what I see as the real value of a network marketing business...a value that goes beyond just the potential of making a lot of money. I finally found a business with a heart and a deep caring for people.

The primary reason I support the industry is that I have always hated the values I found in the traditional educational system. I remember being a junior in high school, about 16 years old, and a teacher told a friend of mine named Martha that she would never amount to much in life because she was not doing well in school. Martha was a shy and sensitive girl. I saw the words of our teacher go straight to her soul. Martha dropped out of school, months short of graduating from high school.

The problem I have with school and the corporate world is that they are similar. It is a survival-of-the-fittest value system. If a person begins to have trouble or cannot understand something, the system simply passes them by. The systems seem to have lost their heart.

While working at Xerox, a friend of mine had three months straight of poor sales. Instead of helping Ron, the sales manager began to threaten, rather than teach, Ron. I can still hear our sales manager saying, "If you don't sell something soon, you'll be fired." Ron resigned a week later.

Therefore, another reason I support the network marketing industry is that in most cases, the companies are very compassionate businesses. If you are willing to stick it out, and learn and study at your own pace, the business will continue to stick by your side. Many network marketing companies are truly equal opportunity businesses. If you will invest the time and effort, so will they. Even though I did not make my fortune in a network marketing business, I will support any business that values human compassion and true equal opportunity.

In Summary

Between the ages of 18 and 27, I was either in a military academy gaining my college education or the U.S. Marine Corps. In those two organizations, the values are truly a *survival-of-the-fittest* value system. At the academy, if you gave the teacher the answers he or she wanted to hear, you graduated. If you didn't, you failed. In the Marine Corps, if you did as you were trained to do, you survived in combat. In war, it truly is survival of the fittest.

When I returned from the Vietnam War, I found myself wanting to change some of my values. I did not want to be good at playing a win/lose...survival-of-the-fittest (or smartest) game we learn at school. That is why richdad.com's mission statement is, "To elevate the financial well-being of humanity." We believe that just because a child does not do well in school, or does not land a high-paying job, does not mean they have to suffer financially all their lives.

Another reason we at richdad.com support many in the network marketing industry is that we feel many, but not all, in the network marketing industry share in the same mission. Today, rather than beat my classmates at test time, or kill my enemy on the battlefield, or wipe out my competition in the corporate world, I would rather work with those who want to help others to achieve their financial goals and dreams without hurting others. For me this is a value worth supporting.

Richdad.com took our *CASHFLOW for Kids* board game and turned it into an interactive game online. The interactive game also comes with a classroom curriculum for ages 5 to 12. This interactive game and curriculum is delivered over the Internet "network" *free of charge* and *free of commercial messages*. It is our way of giving back some of the good fortune we as a business have been blessed to receive. It is also our way of reminding ourselves to be generous rather than greedy.

The fun and entertaining game and curriculum teaches young people throughout the world the same basic financial education and skills my rich dad taught me as a young boy. Years ago, John Lennon of the Beatles taught the world to sing, "Give peace a chance." What we at richdad.com are saying is, "Give all kids a chance." Give all kids the equal opportunity to have a strong basic financial education. We believe that one of the best ways to bring peace is by actively working to end poverty. We also believe the best way to end poverty is by financial education rather than by financial handouts. As my rich dad often said, "If you give a poor person money, you only keep them poor longer."

Today, many network marketing companies are spreading peace through economic opportunity all over the world. Not only are network marketing companies thriving in all the major capitals of the world, but many are also working in the Third World, bringing financial hope to millions of people who live in impoverished countries. Most traditional corporations can only survive where people are rich and have money to spend. It is time that people all over the world have an equal opportunity to enjoy a rich and abundant life, rather than spend their lives working hard only to make the rich richer. If the gap between rich and poor widens, it will be harder to give peace a chance.

The Next Value

The next chapter is about the value of life-changing education that many network marketing companies offer. If you are ready to make financial changes in your life, this next chapter and value is for you.

CHAPTER 4

Value #2: Life-Changing Business Education

It's Not About The Money

"We have the best compensation plan." I often heard this comment when I was investigating different network marketing companies. The people anxious to show me their business opportunity would tell me stories of people making hundreds of thousands of dollars a month because of the business. I have also met people who really do make hundreds of thousands of dollars a month from their network marketing business…so I do not doubt the massive earning potential of a network marketing business.

It is true that the lure of making a lot of money draws many people into this business. Yet I do not recommend looking into a network marketing business primarily for the money.

It's Not About The Products

"We have the best products." This statement is the second most emphasized benefit I was presented with when inspecting different network marketing companies. I also found it interesting how many product-focused companies' sales presentations were based around the life-changing testimonials. In one presentation, the founder of the company told me how she invented her secret potion to save her dying mother in Iowa. After doing some investigation, I found out her mother never lived in Iowa and the product she said she invented came from a laboratory in California that private-labels the product for many other companies. As I said earlier, there are fakes and con men, and in this case con women, in any business and profession.

To be fair, I also found some network marketing companies with great products...some of which I still consume or use today. The point of this chapter is, while great compensation plans and great products are important, they are not the most important aspect of the business to consider.

Many Types Of Businesses To Choose From

In my investigation of different network marketing companies, I was taken by complete surprise at how many different products or services are delivered via a network marketing system.

The first network marketing business opportunity I looked into in the 1970s sold vitamins. I tried them and found them to be excellent quality vitamins. I still take some of those vitamins today. As my search went on, I found network marketing businesses in these mainstream product categories:

1. Cosmetics, skin care and other beauty products
2. Telephone services
3. Real estate services
4. Financial services/insurance/mutual funds/credit cards
5. Legal services
6. Internet market distribution, selling catalogued products at a discount (most everything that Wal-Mart sells)
7. Health care products, vitamins and other wellness related products and services
8. Jewelry
9. Tax services
10. Educational toys

And the list goes on. At least once a month, I hear about a new network marketing company with a new twist on products or on their compensation plan.

It's The Education Plan

The number-one reason I recommend a network marketing business is for its system of education. I recommend investing the time to look past the compensation and products and really look into the heart of the company to see if it is truly interested in training and educating you. That takes more time than just listening to a three-hour sales pitch and looking at colorful product catalogues and how much money people are making. To find out how good their education really is may require you to get off your couch and look into their training, educational seminars and events. If you like what you hear from the initial presentation, take some time to actually meet the people who do the educating and training.

Look carefully, because many network marketing companies say they have great education plans. Yet, I found that some did not have the great education and training systems they claimed they did. In some companies I looked into the only training they had was a recommended book list, and then they focused on training you to recruit your friends and family into the business. So take your time and look carefully because many network marketing companies do have excellent education and training plans…in my opinion, some of the best real-life business training I have seen anywhere.

What To Look For In An Education Plan

If you have read my other books, you already know that I come from a family of educators. My dad was the head of the school system for the State of Hawaii. Although I came from a family of educators, I do not like our traditional education system. Although I received a Congressional Appointment to a prominent federal military academy in New York and graduated with my Bachelor of Science degree, the traditional world of education bored me. I went through the motions of being a student and graduated, but rarely was I challenged or interested in what I was required to study.

After graduating from school, I joined the U.S. Marine Corps and was accepted into the U.S. Navy Flight Program at Pensacola, Florida. The Vietnam War was on and there was an urgent need to train more pilots. While a student pilot, I found the type of education that excited and challenged me. Most of us have heard the overused cliché, "turning caterpillars into butterflies." Well, in flight school, that is exactly what they do. When I entered flight school, I was already a commissioned officer with four years of military training. However, many of the students entering flight school were fresh from civilian colleges and did resemble caterpillars. During the era of the hippies, there were some very strange characters standing there in their civilian clothes, long hair, beards and mustaches, some in sandals rather than shoes, ready to begin a life-changing educational program. If they survived the training, two to three years later they would emerge as butterflies—pilots ready to take on the rigors of some of the toughest flying in the world.

The movie *Top Gun,* starring Tom Cruise, was about the very best of the caterpillars that the U.S. Navy Flight School turned into butterflies. Just before going to Vietnam, I, too, was stationed in San Diego, California where the Top Gun school is located. Although I was not a good enough pilot to be considered for that prestigious school, the energy and confidence displayed by the young pilots in the movie was the way most of us felt as we prepared to go to war. We changed from scruffy young men who could not fly into young men who were trained, disciplined and physically, mentally and emotionally ready to face challenges most people would rather avoid. The change I observed in myself and in my fellow student pilots is what I mean when I say, "life-changing education." Once I finished flight school and left for Vietnam, my life was never the same. I was not the same person who entered flight school.

Years after flight school and the war, many of my fellow pilots went on to become very successful in the world of business. When we get together and re-tell old war stories, we often remark the flight school training had a tremendous impact on our business success.

Therefore, when I speak of life-changing business education, I speak of education powerful enough to change a caterpillar into a butterfly, a process often called a *metamorphosis*. When you look into the educational plan of a network marketing company, I recommend an educational plan that has the power to make that much of a difference in your life.

Yet, I caution you, just as in flight school, not everyone makes it through the program.

Real Life Business School

One of the best things about flight school was that pilots just returning from the war in Vietnam trained us. When they spoke to us, they spoke from real-life experience. One of the problems I had with traditional business school, which I attended for a short period, was that many of the teachers had no real-life business experience. If the teachers did have real-life business experience, it was as employees of a company, mostly middle managers, rather than the founders of the company.

When I attended a traditional business school in Hawaii, going for my M.B.A., I found that I was often attempting to learn some management *theory* or economic *theory* taught by some mid-level manager who worked for a large corporation. If the teacher did not have business experience, the teacher was often someone who had never left the school system. In other words they entered the school system at age 5, entering kindergarten, and were still in the school system trying to teach students about the real-world. To me, that system was a joke.

The reason I went to business school for my M.B.A. was that I wanted to be an entrepreneur, not an employee. Most of the mid-level managers or the teachers on the faculty had no idea what it took to start a business from nothing. Most were not entrepreneurs. Most were employees. Most had no idea what business skills it takes to survive on the streets because not many of them had ever been on the streets of the real-world of business. Most left the ivory towers of school and entered the ivory towers of the corporate world. Most were addicted to job security and to a steady paycheck. In other words, most had great business theories but few had great business skills, skills that would allow them to start a business from nothing and go on to attain great wealth in the real-world of business. Most of them could not survive without a paycheck.

I lasted nine months in that business school and then dropped out never receiving my M.B.A. For me, returning to a traditional business school for my M.B.A. was like returning to a school for caterpillars. After flight school, I wanted to find a business school that taught me to be a butterfly. In 1974 when I was discharged from the Marine Corps, I went to my rich dad and he gave me the business education I was looking for. Rich dad's business school was a business school that focused on the *skills that made a person rich* rather than the *theories of what made a businesses and the economy run*. Rich dad often said, "Skills make you rich, not theories."

"Skills make you rich, not theories."

Do I regret dropping out from business school? Yes, sometimes I do. Yet I am also in good company of dropouts. Bill Gates, Michael Dell, Steve Jobs and Ted Turner were also dropouts. Earlier entrepreneurs such as Thomas Edison and Henry Ford also dropped out of school. I believe that all these entrepreneurs saw the real-world business as a more exciting place to get their real-world business experience. These men became monster butterflies, forever changing the world of business.

Don't get me wrong. Much of the information being taught in the business school I attended was valuable information for anyone in business. However, the school was not teaching me the street-wise skills I knew I needed to be an entrepreneur. Instead, the traditional business school was teaching me the skills to be an employee. Soon after dropping out, I began the first nylon and Velcro surfer wallet business and took it worldwide with over 500 sales reps. By the age of 30, I was a millionaire and then the company went broke two years later. While losing a business was not a pleasant experience, it was a great education. I learned a lot in three years, not only about business, but also about myself.

Building a worldwide business and losing a worldwide business was definitely not an education based on business theory. For me, it was a priceless education, that ultimately made me rich, but more importantly, it was an education that set me free. I did not want an education that would have turned me into a job-seeking caterpillar with an M.B.A. After the crash, rich dad said to me, "Money and success make you arrogant and stupid. Now with some poverty and humility you can become a student again."

The reason I titled this book, *The Business School For People Who Like Helping People,* is because what many network marketing business are. They are business schools for people who want to learn the real-world skills of an entrepreneur, rather than the skills of an employee who wants to become a highly paid mid-level manager in the corporate world.

By attending some of the network marketing businesses trainings, I got to meet the leaders—leaders who were real-world business owners that started their businesses from scratch. Many were great teachers because they were teaching from experience and not from theory. Sitting through many of the business seminars, I often found myself nodding in agreement with their straight talk about what it takes to survive on the streets of the real-world of business. However, more important than teaching just real-world business skills, the leaders taught real-world mental and emotional attitudes that are required to be successful in the world. The education I found in some of the seminars was, priceless...absolutely priceless, especially for anyone who wants to transform into a butterfly.

After the seminars, I would often talk to the instructors. I was amazed at how much money they made not only from their businesses but also from their investments. Several made much more than many top CEOs in corporate America. They definitely made much more than the instructors I had while in a traditional business school.

Yet there was something else to these instructors. Although they were rich and did not have to teach, they had a passion for teaching, for helping their fellow human beings. One reason for their passion is because a network marketing business is based upon the leaders pulling people up, while a traditional corporate or government business is based upon only promoting a few and keeping the masses of employees content with a steady paycheck. These instructors in the network marketing world were *not* saying, "If you don't perform, you lose your job." Instead, they were saying, "Let me help you do better and better." They also would say, "Take as long as you want to learn. As long as you want to learn, I'll be here to teach you. We're on the same team." To me that is the kind of business education I would want.

So when you are looking into a network marketing business seek out the people at the top, the people who are successful in the business, and then ask yourself if you want to learn from them.

Some of the more important real-life business subjects network marketing companies teach are:

1. An attitude of success
2. Leadership skills
3. Communication skills
4. People skills
5. Overcoming personal fears, doubts, and lack of confidence
6. Overcoming the fear of rejection
7. Money management skills
8. Investing skills
9. Accountability skills

10. Time management skills
11. Goal setting
12. Dressing for success

The successful people I have met in the network marketing business have developed these skills from the network marketing training programs. Regardless of whether you reach the top of the network marketing system or make much money, the training is of great value for the rest of your life. If the educational plan is good, it can improve your life for the better, maybe forever.

What Is Life-Changing Education?

The following is the diagram I created to explain what I mean by life-changing education. Notice that it is a tetrahedron, which means a four-sided polyhedron, more commonly known as a pyramid...and the pyramids of Egypt have survived for centuries. In other words, tetrahedrons or pyramids are very stable structures. Scholars have believed for centuries that universal law or nature operates in fours, in this case four sides. That is why there are the four seasons, which are winter, spring, summer, fall. For those who study astrology, there are four primary signs, which are earth, air, fire, and water. When I speak of life-changing education, the changes are again found in the number four. In other words, for true life-changing education to be effective, it must affect all four points of the Learning Pyramid: mental, emotional, physical and spiritual.

The Learning Pyramid

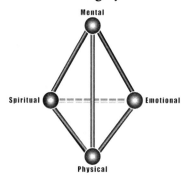

Mental Education

Traditional education focuses primarily on mental education. It teaches you skills such as reading, writing, and arithmetic: all very important skills. These are often called cognitive skills. What I personally did not like about traditional education was how it ignored the emotional, physical, and spiritual aspects of education.

Emotional Education

One of my complaints about traditional education is that it preys on the emotion of fear…more specifically, the fear of making mistakes, which leads to the fear of failing. Instead of inspiring me to learn, the teacher used the fear of failure to motivate me, saying such things as, "If you don't get good grades, you won't get a high-paying job."

In addition, when I was in school, I was punished for making mistakes. In school, I emotionally learned to fear making mistakes. The problem is, in the real-world, the people who get ahead are the people who make the most mistakes and learn from them.

My poor dad, the schoolteacher, thought making a mistake was a sin. My rich dad, on the other hand, said, "Making mistakes is how we are designed to learn. We learn to ride a bicycle by falling off and getting back on again, falling off and getting back on." He also said, "It is a sin to make a mistake and not learn from it."

Explaining further, he said, "The reason so many people lie after making a mistake is because they are emotionally terrified of admitting they made a mistake…hence they waste an opportunity to learn and grow. Making a mistake, admitting it without blaming your mistake on someone else, or justifying or making excuses is how we learn. Making a mistake and not admitting it, or blaming someone else for your mistakes, is a sin." Recently we had a U.S. President who had extra-marital sex in the White House. In my opinion, what was worse than having extra-marital sex was that he lied about the affair when caught. Not only is lying a sign of weak character; it is also a waste of a good mistake—an opportunity to learn something.

In the world of traditional business, the same attitude toward mistakes prevails. In the world of business, if you make a mistake, you are often fired or punished. In the world of network marketing, you are encouraged to learn by making mistakes, correcting, and getting smarter mentally as well as emotionally. When I was learning to sell in the corporate world, the sales people who underachieved were fired. In other words, we live in a world of fear of failing, not of learning. That is why so many people in the corporate world remain caterpillars. How can a person fly when they live in a corporate cocoon wrapped tightly with the fear of failing?

In the world of network marketing, the leader's focus is to work with those who are not doing well and to encourage them to move up, not to fire them. You would probably never have learned to ride a bicycle if you were punished for falling off and given a failing grade in bicycle riding.

I am more financially successful than most people, not because I was smarter than most people, but because I failed more than most people. In other words, I got ahead because I made more mistakes. In network marketing, you are encouraged to make mistakes, correct, learn and grow. To me that is life-changing education. When you let go of your fear you can begin to fly.

If you are a person who is terrified of making mistakes and afraid of failing, then I believe a network marketing business with a great educational program is especially good for you. I have witnessed network marketing training programs that build and restore a person's self-confidence...and once you have more confidence, your life is changed forever.

Physical Education

Simply put, people afraid of making mistakes don't learn much because they don't do much. Most people know that learning is really a physical process as much as it is a mental process. Reading and writing are physical processes, just as learning to play tennis is a physical process. If you have been conditioned to know all the right answers and not to make mistakes, the chances are your educational process is hampered. How can you progress if you know all the answers but are terrified of trying anything?

The network marketing companies I have studied all encourage physical learning as much as they encourage mental learning. They encourage you to go out and face your fears by taking action, making a mistake, learning from the mistake, and growing mentally, emotionally and physically stronger from the process.

Traditional education encourages you to learn the facts and then emotionally teaches you to be afraid of making mistakes, which holds you back physically. Living in an environment of fear is not healthy, mentally, emotionally, physically or financially. As I have stated before, I have more money not because I am academically smarter, but because I made more mistakes, admitted to making the mistake, and learned my lessons from the mistakes. I then went on to make more mistakes...and I am looking forward to making more mistakes in the future...while most people are working hard to make no more mistakes in their future...which is why we have different futures. You cannot improve your future if you are not willing to try something new and risk making mistakes and learning from them.

The best network marketing companies encourage their people to learn something new mentally, take action, make mistakes, learn, correct and repeat the process. That is real-life education.

If you are afraid of making mistakes, but know you need to make some changes in your life, then a good network marketing program could be the best long-term personal development program for you. A good network marketing company will take you by the hand and guide you to a life beyond fear and failing. In addition, if you don't want your hand held, they won't hold it.

It has been said that if you want to change what a person does, change the way they *think*. Lately, more people are subscribing to the idea that if you want to change the way a person *thinks,* first change what they are *doing*. The great thing about a network marketing business is that it focuses on both what you *think* and what you *do.*

The trouble with traditional educational systems is that they punish you for doing the wrong thing, rather than correcting what you are doing.

Spiritual Education

First, I feel it important that I explain my personal views before going into this often hot and emotional topic. I use the word spiritual versus religious for specific reasons. Just as there are good network marketing companies and bad network marketing companies, in my opinion there are good religious organizations and bad religious organizations. More specifically, I have seen religious organizations strengthen a person spiritually, and I have seen other religious organizations weaken a person spiritually.

Therefore, when I speak of spiritual education, it may or may not include religious education. When I speak of spiritual education, I speak non-denominationally. When it comes to religion, I support the *Constitution of the United States of America,* which grants the freedom of religious choice.

The reason I am cautious about this subject is that I was told at an early age, "Never discuss religion, politics, sex, and money." In addition, I agree with that statement simply because these subjects can be volatile and emotional. It is not my intent to offend your personal feelings or beliefs but to support your rights to have them.

Beyond Human Limitations

When I speak of a person's spirit, I speak of the power that propels us past our mental, emotional and physical limitations…limitations that often define our human condition.

While I was in Vietnam, I saw young men wounded who knew they were dying, yet they continued to fight on so others could live. A classmate from school that fought behind enemy lines for most of his time in Vietnam said it most accurately when he said, "I am alive today because dead men kept fighting." He went on to say, "Twice I was in battles where I was the only one to come out alive. Your life changes when you realize that your friends gave their lives so you could live."

On nights before a battle, I would sit at the bow of the aircraft carrier silently as the waves passed below. In these long moments of silence, I made peace with my soul. I realized that in the morning I would face death again. It was during one of these long evenings of quiet and solitude that I realized that to die the next day was the easy way out. I realized that living was in many ways much harder than dying. Once I was at peace with the possibility of either life or death, I could then choose how I wanted to live my life the next day. In other words, would I fly with courage or would I fly with fear? Once I made my choice, I called on my human spirit to carry me through the next day, to fly and fight to the best of my ability, regardless of the outcome.

War is a horrible event. It causes people to do horrible things to other human beings. Yet it was in war that I also saw the very best of humanity. It was in war that I gained a sense of human power far beyond our human limitations. Moreover, we all have that power. I know you have it.

The good news is that you don't have to go to war to witness this power. One day while watching a track meet of physically challenged young girls and boys, the same human spirit touched me. When I saw young people, some without legs, sprinting with prosthetic legs, running with all their heart and soul, their spirit touched my spirit. Tears came to my eyes as I watched one young girl with only one leg running with all her heart. I could see on her face the pain caused by running on her replacement leg; yet her physical pain was no match for the power of her spirit. Although she did not win the race, she won my heart. She touched my human spirit and reminded me of what I had forgotten. At that moment, I realized that all these young people were running for all of us as much as they were running for themselves.

We are often reminded of the power of our spirit in movies. In the movie *Brave Heart,* Mel Gibson rides in front of his ragtag band of Scottish farmers, terrified by the powerful British Army in front of them, and bellows from his soul, "They can kill our bodies, but they can't take our freedom." At that moment, he is speaking from his human spirit to theirs. By touching their spirits, he was overpowering their emotions of fear and doubt caused by lack of training and inferior weapons. He ignited their spirits to go on and defeat the most powerful army in the world.

I have noticed that the successful leaders in network marketing have been trained to develop this ability to speak to the human spirit. They have the ability to touch the greatness in those coming behind them and to inspire them to move up…to go beyond their human limitations, go beyond their doubts and fears. That is the power of life-changing education.

My rich dad often said to me, especially in times when I was out of money, out of self-confidence, and out of answers, "There are three people in all of us. There is a rich person, a poor person, and a middle-class person. It is your job to find out which ones come out." Rich dad also said, "The world of business and investing is made up of two emotions. They are greed and fear. The reason that most people are not rich is not because of greed, it is because of fear. If you want to become rich, you need to overcome your fear and fly." In my opinion, the best way to overcome your fears is by getting you back in touch with your spirit and that is what many network marketing companies do.

The word education means to *draw out*. One of the problems I have with traditional education was that it is based on the fear of failing rather than the challenges of learning from our mistakes. In my opinion, traditional education is designed to draw out the middle-class person in us...the person that feels insecure, needs a job, a steady paycheck, lives in fear of making mistakes, and worries about what their friends might think of them if they do something different. The reason I support most of the network marketing companies and I titled this book, *The Business School For People Who Like Helping People,* is that the kind of education I found in network marketing companies was education that was designed to *draw out* the rich person in you. I value that kind of life-changing education.

By the way, *Forbes* magazine defines a rich person as someone who earns $1 million or more per year. A poor person is defined as someone who earns less than $25,000 a year. The question is not what you earn today. The question is, "Is your job training you to earn over $1million a year or more?" If not, you may want to seek better education.

In Summary

When I lost my first company, the nylon and Velcro surfer wallet business, my rich dad congratulated me. He said, "You've just paid for a multi-million dollar education. You're on your way to becoming very rich." He also said, "The reason most people never find the rich person inside of them is because the poor person still thinks it's bad to make mistakes."

To me the difference between the values found in *traditional* education and the value found in life-changing education is the difference between the values placed on learning from our mistakes versus punishing people for making mistakes, and placing value on the human spirit—a spirit powerful enough to overcome any lack of mental, emotional or physical talents.

The Next Value

My poor dad valued job security. My rich dad valued financial freedom. In the next chapter, we will discuss the value of changing from a person who seeks job security to a person who seeks financial freedom. It begins by changing quadrants. In other words, you will find out why changing jobs is not life-changing.

CHAPTER 5

Value #3: Friends Who Will Pull You Up, Not Push You Down

"What will my friends say?" is a question or concern I heard many times while attending the educational seminars put on by a network marketing company. "They'll think I'm crazy" is another often-heard concern.

For many people, even though the business opportunity made sense and they wanted to make changes in their financial lives, one of the biggest hurdles of all was what their friends and family would think if they started a network marketing business.

One evening, there was a single mom standing in front of a group of about 30 guests who came to hear about the business opportunity she found in network marketing. The single mom was telling everyone about how her husband left, leaving her with the job of raising four children on her own. Rather than go on welfare, this brave young mother told the group about how she started a network marketing business and was today earning over $60,000 a year part-time, raising her young children full-time. She told the group that the business had given her security, hope, control of her life and most importantly, time with her kids. In closing she said, "On top of that, in 10 more years I'll be a millionaire because the business keeps growing. I could never have done that if I had kept my old job. I could never have done that without the support of the people in this business."

For her, the money was not the most important thing. For her, the business had given her life back. She could once again dream dreams she had dared not dream for years. In a question-and-answer period, she said, "I can provide the college education for my kids, and they will not need to take care of me when I'm older. I will not be a burden to them. That is such a relief. That is such peace of mind."

As the evening broke up, I thanked the person who was in the business who invited me. Walking out the door I was asked by a young male business executive, who was also a guest, "What did you think?"

"I thought it was a great presentation," I replied.

"Yes it was. But it sounds too good to be true," he said as he searched for his keys in his briefcase.

"Why don't you invest a little time and find out if it is true or not?" I suggested. "It might be just what you're looking for."

"No, I couldn't do that. Do you know what my friends back at the office would think if I told them I was starting a network marketing business? They'd laugh their heads off. You know how guys are."

Nodding, I smiled and replied, "Yes I know how guys are." He climbed in his car, I climbed in mine, and we drove off into the night.

The Hardest Job Of All

In 1976, my nylon and Velcro surfer wallet was launched. Two friends and I had started it from scratch, part-time, while working full-time for Xerox. I knew I could not stay with Xerox for long because the surfer wallet business was beginning to take off and more and more time was required. I can still remember telling a few of the people at the office that I would soon have to quit my job at Xerox and run the surfer wallet business full-time.

"You're crazy!" said one of the more senior salespersons. "You're going to fail."

"You know how many people want to work for Xerox?" said another senior salesperson. "You have a great job, great benefits, good pay and lots of promotion opportunities. If you keep your nose clean, someday you could be a sales manager. Why would you risk losing such a great job?"

"You'll be back," said another salesperson. "I've seen countless people like you. People who think they're hot shots. They leave the company, fail and come back with their tail between their legs…if they have any tail left."

The group of six salesmen and two saleswomen laughed with that comment and went on talking about the new copier the company was coming out with, and after that they talked about who was going to win the baseball game that night. I realized I had talked to the wrong people about my business and about my dreams. I realized I was talking to people who would pull me down rather than push me up.

Years later, after the network marketing meeting when that young man said to me, "No, I couldn't do that. You know what my friends back at the office would think if I told them I was starting a network marketing business.

They'd laugh their heads off. You know how people are." I knew exactly what he was talking about.

For me, the hardest part of leaving a secure job and starting a business was dealing with what my friends, family and co-workers would say or think. For me, that was the hardest job of all.

A Change Of Quadrants, Not A Change Of Jobs

How many times have you heard people say some of the following statements?

1. "I wish I could quit my job."
2. "I'm tired of going from job to job."
3. "I wish I could make more money, but I can't afford to quit and start all over with a new company. And I don't want to go back to school and learn a new profession."
4. "Every time I get a pay raise, most of my raise is eaten up by taxes."
5. "I'm working hard, but the only people getting rich are the owners of the company."
6. "I'm working hard, but I'm not getting ahead financially. I've got to start thinking about retirement."
7. "I'm afraid technology or a younger worker will make me obsolete."
8. "I can't keep working this hard. I'm getting too old for this."
9. "I went to dental school to be a dentist, but I don't want to be a dentist anymore."
10. "I just want to do something different and meet new people. I'm tired of wasting my time, hanging around people without much ambition and who aren't going anywhere. I'm tired of spending time with people who work just hard enough...so they won't be fired, and I'm also tired of working for a company that pays us just enough...so we won't quit."

These are often statements made by individuals trapped in one of the quadrants of the CASHFLOW Quadrant. These are comments often made by people ready to change quadrants. Unfortunately, rather than change quadrants, they just change jobs.

What Is The CASHFLOW Quadrant?

My second book in the Rich Dad series is *Rich Dad's CASHFLOW Quadrant*. Many people say that it is my most important book, especially for people ready to make changes in their life...a change far greater than simply going from job to job.

The diagram below is my rich dad's CASHFLOW Quadrant.

The E stands for "employee."
The S stands for "self-employed" or "small business owner."
The B stands for "business owner."
The I stands for "investor."

How Do You Know Which Quadrant You Are In?

The way you know which quadrant you are in is simply from which quadrant your cash flows. For example, if you receive your income from a job and you receive a regular paycheck from a company or business *you do not own,* then your cash flows out of the E quadrant. If you receive the bulk of your money from your investments, then you are an investor, a person from the I quadrant. If you are a small business owner, a specialist such as a doctor or lawyer, a commission-only person such as a real estate agent, then you are probably in the S quadrant. In addition, if you own a big business, a company or business that employs over 500 people, then you are in the B quadrant.

Different Quadrants, Different Values

Years ago, rich dad explained to me that different quadrants had different values. For example, even though a person in the E quadrant can be a janitor or the president of the company, they are united by the same set of core values. A person in the E quadrant, regardless if they are the janitor or the president, often thinks or says words such as, "I am looking for a safe, secure job with benefits." Or, "How much do we get for overtime?" Or, "How many paid holidays do we have?" In other words, *security* is a very important core value for someone in the E quadrant.

S Quadrant Values

For people in the S quadrant the core value is *independence*. They want their freedom and do what they want. When a person says, "I'm going to quit my job and go out on my own," they are often heading from the E quadrant to the S quadrant.

People found in the S quadrant are small business owners, mom and pop businesses, specialists and consultants. For example, I have a friend who installs big screen televisions, phone systems and security systems for rich people's homes. He has a staff of three and is happy to be the boss of just three people. He is a hardcore, hard-working S. Commissioned sales people such as real estate and insurance brokers are in the S quadrant. The S quadrant is also filled with professional people such as doctors, lawyers and accountants who do not belong to a large medical, legal, or accounting firm.

The way you know a person in the S quadrant is, again, by their words. An S quadrant person will often say, "If you want something done right, do it yourself." Or, "I have the best products." If they had a theme song, it would be, "Nobody does it better." At the core of the S, behind the facade of independence, is often a lack of trust of other people...trust that someone can do it better than they can.

The way an S gets paid is often by commission or by the amount of time they spend on a job. For example, an S may be heard saying words such as, "My commission is 6 percent of the total purchase price." Or, "I charge $100 an hour." Or, "My fee is cost plus 10 percent."

The S quadrant person is the John Wayne of business. You can hear them saying, "I'm going to do it on my own."

B Quadrant Values

People who start from nothing and build great B quadrant businesses are often people with powerful life missions, value a great team and efficient team-work, and want to serve and work with as many people as possible. Earlier in this book, I mentioned Thomas Edison, founder of General Electric; Henry Ford, founder of Ford Motor Company; and Bill Gates, founder of Microsoft, all of whom are B's.

While a person in the S quadrant wants to be the best in their field, a B quadrant person often is looking for other people who are the best in their field to join his or her team. Henry Ford surrounded himself with people smarter than he was. An S quadrant businessperson is often the smartest person on a small team, for example a doctor or a consultant.

When it comes to being paid, a true B quadrant person can leave his or her business and still get paid. In most cases, if someone in the S quadrant stops working, their income stops also. Therefore, a question you may want to ask yourself now is, "If I stop working today, how much income continues to come in?" If your income stops in six months or less, then chances are, you are in the E or S quadrants. A person in the B or I quadrants can stop working for years and the money will continue to come in.

I Quadrant Values

The I quadrant values *financial freedom.* The investor loves the idea of their money working instead of them working.

Investors invest in many things. They may invest in gold coins, real estate, businesses, or paper assets such as stocks, bonds and mutual funds.

If your income comes from company or government retirement plans, rather than your own personal investing knowledge, then that is income from the E quadrant. In other words, your boss or the business is still paying its bill for your years of service.

Words an investor might be heard saying are, "I'm receiving a 20 percent return on my assets," or, "Show me the company's financials," or, "How much deferred maintenance is on the property?"

Different Quadrants, Different Investors

In today's world, we all need to be investors. However, our school systems do not teach us much about investing. Oh, I know that some schools teach stock picking, but to me that is not investing. To me picking stocks is gambling, not investing.

Years ago, rich dad pointed out to me that most employees invest in mutual funds or savings. He also said, "Doctors are often the worst investors." He also said, "Just because you're successful in one quadrant, such as the E, S, or B, does not mean you will be successful in the I quadrant."

Rich dad also pointed out to me that different quadrants invest in different ways. For example, a person in the S quadrant might be heard saying, "I don't invest in real estate because I don't want to fix toilets." A person in the B quadrant addressing the same investment challenge might say, "I want to hire a property management company to fix my toilets at night." In other words, an S quadrant investor will think they have to do the property maintenance on their own and a B quadrant investor will hire another company to do their property maintenance for them. Different people, different mindsets, different quadrants, different values.

If you would like to find out more about the different people who are attracted to the different quadrants, you may want to read book number two in the Rich Dad series, *Rich Dad's CASHFLOW Quadrant,* for greater insights. As stated earlier, many people say *CASHFLOW Quadrant* is the most important book for people ready to make changes in their lives.

A Network Marketing Business Is A B Quadrant Business

A network marketing business is for people who want to enter the world of the B quadrant. Why is it a B quadrant business? The answer is because the network marketing business system is designed to expand to well over 500 people. Also, the income potential in a network marketing business is, in theory, while the income potential for the E and S quadrants are often limited to how much you as an individual can produce. In a network marketing business, you can earn as much as your network can earn. If you build a big network, you can earn a massive amount of money.

After you have built a large network marketing business, the next step is to move from the B quadrant to the I quadrant. At least that is what my rich dad recommended I do, and that is what I did. My fellow salespersons who scoffed at me leaving Xerox and starting my own business are still salespersons today. They never changed their mindset, their core values, and hence they never changed their quadrant. Today I know some of them are worried about losing their jobs and a few of them do not have enough money for retirement. In other words, they spent too much time in the E and S quadrants.

What Do You Want To Be When You Grow Up?

When I was a kid, my poor dad often said, "Go to school and get good grades so you can get a safe secure job." He was programming me for the E quadrant.

My mother often said, "If you want to be rich, you should become a doctor or lawyer. That way you'll always have a profession to fall back on." She was programming me for the S quadrant.

My rich dad said, "If you want to be rich, you should mind your own business." Rich dad recommended I learn to become a business owner and an investor.

When I returned from Vietnam, I had to make up my mind on which dad I would listen to. Looking at the CASHFLOW Quadrant,

I had to ask myself this question: "In which quadrant do I have the most chance of financial success?" Knowing that I did not want to be an employee all my life, nor did I want to go to school to become a doctor or lawyer in the S quadrant, I knew that my best chances were in the B and I quadrants. I knew the B and I quadrants were best for me simply because I wanted to be a multi-millionaire and I did not want to take orders or work hard all my life in order to earn those millions of dollars. Today, I earn millions of dollars without having to go to work or work harder and harder. I work less and earn more because I use the power of networks.

Now it is *your turn* to look at the quadrants. The question you may want to ask yourself is, "Which quadrant or quadrants are best for me?"

One of the reasons many people fail to become successful in their lives is because they do not change quadrants...most people only change jobs. That is why you hear of people going from job to job, or people saying, "I've found the perfect job." Even if they find the perfect job, they haven't changed much because they haven't changed quadrants.

A Change Of Quadrants Means A Change Of Values And Friends

One of the advantages of a network marketing business is that the business is filled with new people, some of which may become your new best friends. For me the hardest part of leaving Xerox was that most of my friends and family were in the E quadrant. They had different values than I did. They valued security and a steady paycheck and I valued freedom and financial independence.

If you are considering making a change of quadrants and are considering a network marketing business, you have a tremendous advantage over me. At least a network marketing business provides a large support group of like-minded people—people with the same core values, the values of the B quadrant—to assist you while you make your transition. All I had was my rich dad and his son to encourage me. Everyone else thought I was crazy, and maybe I was. However, to stay at the Xerox Corporation just because I needed job security and a steady paycheck was not enough of a reason for me to stay there.

The friends I left behind at Xerox are still great friends. They will always be great friends because they were there for me at a transition phase of my life. However, for me it was time to move on. If it is time for you to move on and the B quadrant is calling you, you may want to join a network marketing business and begin to meet new friends.

Which Quadrant Are Your Friends In?

Today, I have friends in all four quadrants. Yet my core friends are in the B and

I quadrants. One of the challenges in communicating between people is that I am always aware of their values and their quadrant. I have noticed that when I talk about business or investing to a person in the E quadrant, they do not fully understand me or what I say frightens them. For example, if I say to someone in the E quadrant, "I love starting my own businesses." They may reply, "Isn't that risky?" The point I am making is that we are speaking from different core values. What is exciting for me is frightening to someone else. So rather than frighten those in the E and S quadrants, I talk about the weather, sports, or what is on television.

Many people who are already in the network marketing business use my rich dad's CASHFLOW Quadrant as a way of explaining their business. They will draw the quadrant as I have below:

They will then explain the differences in core values to a person who might be interested in starting their network marketing business. Many of them report that by using this diagram, the potential new business owner finds it more comforting and more understandable. The new person has a chance to understand that they are making core value changes and are entering a business school to learn how to be a business owner rather than an employee.

While not all people will start a business, many people will appreciate your use of the quadrant, addressing the core values, and offering them time to make up their mind, rather than the hard sales pressure to start a business. If you will take time to look at the quadrant and weigh the pros and cons, I think you will know that making the change from one quadrant to another is more than a change of mind; it really is a change of core values, and changing values often takes time.

"Changing from one quadrant to another is a change of core values."

One of the reasons I believe network marketing is so difficult to explain is simply because there are very few people who are successful in the B quadrant. Most people, due to our schools and family values, are in either the E or S quadrants. In fact, I would estimate that 80 percent of the population is in the E or S quadrant. I would also say 15 percent are in the I quadrant and that less than 5 percent of the population are genuinely in the B quadrant. In other words, there are very few Thomas Edison's and Bill Gates' running around the planet. Many famous CEOs are E quadrant people, not B quadrant people. For example, the famous Jack Welch, former CEO of General Electric, was still an employee of General Electric. Granted, he was a brilliant leader, but the business owner, the founder of GE, was a school dropout named Thomas Edison. Edison had the vision and the drive to start something from nothing and turn it into a giant business.

Repeating what I have said, very few people have actually been around a true B quadrant leader. Therefore, when people come to hear about a business opportunity from a network marketing business leader, they often have no idea how big an opportunity they are looking at. Being around Es and Ss most of their lives has not allowed them the luxury of thinking that big, so many fail to see the true size of the opportunity being offered. At an early age, I was fortunate enough to have my rich dad to expand my mind to the power of a B quadrant business. That is why I have only had a job for four years of my life. I had no plans on being an E or an S when I grew up. I knew the quadrants I wanted to live in were the B and I quadrants.

If you decide to start a network marketing business and are talking to a friend, take the time to explain to them the quadrants and why you made your own personal quadrant change. If you take the time to explain the quadrants to them, they may be far more supportive than if you just blurt out, "I am starting a part-time business with a network marketing company." As I said, the reason the business is often so hard to explain is that so few people know anyone in the B quadrant. All most people have around them are E and S quadrant friends and family. So be patient and use the quadrants to explain your new perspective on life. In addition, who knows, if you are patient and do a good job explaining the changes you are going through, they might just join you on your journey. Just let them know that the journey is a process, not a get-rich-quick-scheme, and the journey may take years. If you are serious, I recommend a five-year plan.

Five-Year Plan

I am often asked, "Why a five-year plan?" The following are my reasons.

Reason #1: It took years for Starbucks to be built. It took years for McDonalds to be built. It was years before Sony became an entertainment giant. In other words, it takes years to build great companies and great business leaders. Most people do not think in terms of years. Most people think in terms of immediate gratification and getting rich quick. That is why there are so few people in the B quadrant. Most people want money but are unwilling to invest their time.

As stated earlier, learning is a physical process...and physical learning sometimes takes longer than just mental learning. For example, you may decide to learn to ride a bicycle, but the physical learning process may take longer than the mental decision to learn to ride a bicycle. The good news is that once you learn physically, you generally have learned something forever.

Reason #2: On the other side, unlearning is also a physical process. There is a statement that goes, "You can't teach an old dog new tricks." Well thankfully, we are humans and not dogs. Yet there is some truth to the idea that the older we get, it is sometimes harder to unlearn things we have spent years learning. One of the reasons so many people feel more comfortable in the E and S quadrants is because they feel comfortable and secure there. After all, they spent years learning how to be there. So, many people return there because it is comfortable, even though that comfort is not good for them in the end.

Take your time to both unlearn as well as learn. For some people, the hardest part of switching from the left side of the Quadrant to the right side of the Quadrant is to unlearn the point of view of the E and S quadrants. Once you have unlearned what you have learned, I think the change will go much faster and easier.

Reason #3: All caterpillars make a cocoon before becoming butterflies. Flight school was my cocoon. I entered flight school as a college graduate and exited flight school, a pilot ready to go to Vietnam. If I had gone to a civilian flight school, I doubt if I would have been ready for war even though I was a pilot. What we had to learn as military pilots is different from what civilian pilots have to learn. The skills are different, the intensity of training is different, and the reality of going to war at the end of the training makes things different.

It took me nearly two years to get through basic flight school in Florida. I received my wings, which meant I was a pilot, and I was then transferred to advanced flight training at Camp Pendleton, California. There we were trained to fight more than to fly. I will not bore you with the details, but at Camp Pendleton, the training escalated in intensity.

After we had finished flight school and became pilots, we had one year to prepare to go to Vietnam. To prepare, we flew constantly, flying in conditions that tested us mentally, emotionally, physically and spiritually...again all four points of the Learning Pyramid.

About eight months into the program at Camp Pendleton, something changed inside of me. During one training flight, I finally became a pilot who was ready to go to war. Up to that point in time, I was flying mentally, emotionally and physically. Some people call it "flying mechanically." On that one training mission, I changed spiritually. The mission was so intense and frightening that suddenly, all my doubts and fears were forced out of the way, and my human spirit took over. Flying had become a part of me. I felt at peace and at home inside the aircraft. The aircraft was part of me. I was ready to go to Vietnam.

It was not that I had no fear...for I did. The same fear about going to war was still there. The same fear of dying or, even worse, becoming crippled was still there. The difference was that I was now ready to go to war. My confidence in myself was greater than the fears. In addition, this same type of life-changing education is found in many network marketing businesses.

My process of becoming a businessperson and investor has followed much the same process as becoming a pilot ready to go into battle. It took my failing twice in business before I suddenly found my spirit...a spirit often called the "entrepreneurial spirit." It is a spirit that keeps me on the B and I side no matter how tough things get. I stay on the B and I side rather than slipping back to the safety and comfort of the E and S side. I would say it took me 15 years to gain the confidence to feel comfortable in the B quadrant.

I Still Use The Five-Year Plan

When I decide to learn something new, for example, investing in real estate, I still allow myself five years to learn the process. When I wanted to learn how to invest in stocks, I again gave myself five years to learn the process. Many people invest once, lose a few dollars, and then quit. They quit after their first mistake, which is why they fail to learn. My rich dad would say, "A true winner knows that losing is part of the process of winning. It is only the losers of life who think the winners never lose. A loser is someone who dreams of winning and does everything possible to avoid making mistakes."

Today I still give myself five years to make as many mistakes as possible. I do this because I know that the more mistakes I make and learn from...the smarter I will be in five years. If I make no mistakes for five years, then I am no smarter than I was five years ago. I am only five years older.

My Journey In The B And I Quadrants Has Not Ended

Personally, I have been on the journey for years and I still have lots to learn. I will probably be on the journey for the rest of my life. The good thing is the more I learn, the more I earn and the less I have to work. If you or your friends have the idea that you can start a network marketing business and expect to start making money right away then you are still thinking like a person from the E or S quadrants. People in the E and S quadrants are the ones who most often are sucked into the get rich quick schemes and scams of life. If you are serious about starting your journey, I would recommend committing to a minimum of five years of learning, growing, changing your core values and meeting new friends. To me, those changes are far more important than a few extra bucks.

In Summary

In summary, the advantage of a network marketing business is that not only does the business provide a great business education, the business often provides a whole new world of friends—friends who are going in the same direction as you and share the same core values as you do. To me, that kind of friendship is priceless. I know that I would not have made the journey if I had not met some great friends along the way.

P.S. If you should use the CASHFLOW Quadrant in your explanations, I would appreciate it if you gave credit to my rich dad for coming up with such a simple explanation of the four different people found in the world of money, business and life. Years ago, my rich dad's quadrant showed me the way to a world my poor dad did not know existed. I hope the quadrant does the same for you.

What Quadrants Are You, Your Friends, And Your Family In?

Before moving on to the next chapter, you may want to take a moment to assess those closest to you and their quadrants.

Person	**Quadrant (E, S, B or I)**
Father	_____
Mother	_____
Spouse	_____
Brothers *(list by name)*	
_____	_____
_____	_____
Sisters *(list by name)*	
_____	_____
_____	_____

Friends *(list by name)*

——————————   ——————————
——————————   ——————————
——————————   ——————————
——————————   ——————————
——————————   ——————————
——————————   ——————————

What quadrant are you in today and which quadrant(s) do you want to be in tomorrow?

	E	S	B	I
Your Quadrant Today	——	——	——	——
Your Quadrant Tomorrow	——	——	——	——

What is your plan to change quadrants? How do you plan to gain the education, experience, and change in core values?

_____

_____

_____

_____

_____

_____

The Next Value

The next chapter contains the value of building a network of friends who become business owners.

CHAPTER 6

Value #4: What Is The Value Of A Network?

In 1974, while working for the Xerox Corporation in Hawaii, I was having a difficult time selling a product known as the Xerox telecopier. I was having trouble selling the telecopier because it was a new product. Not only was it a relatively new product, but a commonly asked question was, "Well, who else has one?" In other words, having a telecopier had no value without someone else having a telecopier...a network of other telecopiers. Today most people have never heard of a telecopier, but most people heard of a fax machine.

As more and more people began using these new fax machines, the value of the telecopier went up, and sales became much easier. I spent four years struggling to sell these new machines, investing a lot of time explaining what they were and how a business could use one. Today every business and many homes have one. Today, instead of spending hours trying to explain the benefits of a telecopier, people just choose the model they want. Very little explanation is needed except on how to use the machine. The point of this discussion is that the value of telecopier, or fax machine, went up in value once it became a network. That is why this chapter is on the value or the power of a network.

Metcalf's Law

Robert Metcalf is one of the people credited for creating the Ethernet. He also more recently founded the technology company 3Com Corp. He is also credited for defining Metcalf's Law, which is:

A Network's Economic Value = Number of Users^2

Stating Metcalf's Law in simpler terms, If there exists just one telephone, that single telephone really has no economic value. The moment there are two telephones, according to Metcalf's Law, the economic value of the phone network is now squared. The economic value of the network would go from zero to two (squared) or four. Add a third phone and the economic value of the network is now nine. In other words, the economic value of a network goes up exponentially, not numerically.

> **"The economic value of a network goes up exponentially, not numerically."**

The John Wayne Businessman

During my father's generation, John Wayne was the role model for success. John Wayne portrayed the rugged individual who needed no one else to get the job done. Even the way John Wayne treated women was in the "Me Tarzan...you Jane" stereotype of relationships. Television programs during that period, such as *Leave It To Beaver,* showed Ward Cleaver (Beaver's father) going off to work with June Cleaver (Beaver's mother) waiting at home, being the dutiful wife, cooking and cleaning until her *knight in shining armor*—her husband—came home with the paycheck.

While many things have changed since those 1950s movies and television shows, many old business ideas from that era still exist. Today, I still hear people say, "I'm going into business and I'm going to do it on my own." To me, the *doing it on your own* idea is the John Wayne idea of how to get into business. Earlier I wrote that when most people say they are going into business to *do their own thing,* they often move from the E quadrant into the S quadrant rather than the B quadrant. Today the S quadrant is the home of the rugged individual, the John Wayne quadrant of business.

A Franchise Is A Network

In the 1950s a new type of business model began to emerge, a business model known as a *franchise.* Some of the more famous names in franchising are McDonalds, Wendy's, etc. Today franchises are widely accepted. Yet back in the 1950s many old-thinking business people—the John Wayne's of business—criticized franchises, some even calling them illegal. Today, wherever I travel the world, I see the famous franchises such as McDonalds in Beijing, South Africa, and in very remote places. Today the world has embraced franchises.

Simply put, a franchise is a form of business network made up of multiple business owners working together. Today we all know a McDonald's franchise owner has much more horsepower than the rugged individual who starts his or her own hamburger stand. If a McDonald's locates near the rugged individual's independent hamburger stand, chances are the rugged individual is soon out of business even though John Wayne can fry a better hamburger.

As in any new business startup, a new franchise is not very valuable until it has more and more franchisees. I remember seeing the first Mail Boxes Etc. and wondering what it was. Suddenly the company had explosive growth through adding franchises. The same is true with Starbucks. Years ago, I began hearing about this tiny coffee company with a funny name that operated coffee carts in Seattle. Today I see Starbucks everywhere I go. In New York, they seem to have a Starbucks on every corner. While this incredible growth has been primarily through company-owned stores, not franchises, this is another example of Metcalf's Law at work.

In my neighborhood, a small packaging and mail shop that had been in business for years was forced out of business when a Mail Boxes Etc. franchise opened up in the same shopping center. The same thing happened to a small coffee shop operator. The small coffee shop went out of business, losing to Starbucks, even though the small coffee shop had great coffee. Again, the rugged individual loses to the networker.

The Second Type Of Networked Business

In the 1970s, a new type of networked business began to take off. That business is the business this book is about, a networked business that today is known as network marketing. Instead of a network of franchised businesses, it is a network of franchised individuals. In other words, it's a personal franchise. This new type of networked business has also come under much criticism when it first became popular and millions of people began to get into the business. The business continues to be criticized. Yet in spite of all the criticism, the network marketing industry continues to grow faster than franchises or traditional big businesses.

One of the reasons most people cannot see the rapid growth of network marketing is simply because network marketing is in most cases an invisible business. Unlike signs that shout McDonalds or Starbucks, most network marketing franchises operate discreetly out of homes or small offices. On top of that, many successful network-marketing franchises make far more money than most franchises.

Big Business Is Now In The Network Marketing Business

At the start of this book, I listed some of the products or services that are now delivered through a network marketing distribution system. This list includes products such as legal services, tax services, telephone services, cosmetics, vitamins, clothing and even real estate. One of the more surprising things I found out once I opened my mind is the number of major corporations such as Citibank, AOL Time Warner and Berkshire Hathaway that have network marketing business operations. Once I opened my mind, I realized that I had only been hearing the criticisms of network marketing from people who were not in the business. I could not see the business as it is truly a virtual business, which means it is invisible, so I could not see the growth of the industry. I could only hear the complaints from old-style business people, or the John Waynes of business. The reason the industry continues to grow is the power found in Metcalf's Law.

Harness The Power Of Metcalf's Law

The beauty of network marketing is that it has made available to the average individual—people like you and me—the power of Metcalf's Law...but you must obey the law. If you follow the principle of the law, just affiliating with a network marketing company is a good start, but that act alone does not entitle you to harness the power. It would be like you buying a telephone, but you are the only one with the telephone.

> **"Your job is to clone or duplicate someone just like you."**

In order for you to harness the power, your job is to clone or duplicate someone just like you. The moment there are two of you, your economic value is squared. The value of your network has just gone from zero to four. The moment there are three of you, the economic value of your network goes from four to nine. If the two people you bring in also develop two more people each, the economic value of your network begins to look like a rocket taking off for the moon. Instead of working hard numerically, your economic value begins to grow exponentially. That is the power and the value of a networked business.

Over time, a successful networker has the potential to out-earn most professional people such as doctors, lawyers, accountants, and other rugged individuals. The difference and the power are explained through Metcalf's Law: a very important value of a network marketing business.

In the previous chapter, I talked about the value of new friends. If you will invest a little time and explain to them the CASHFLOW Quadrant, asking them which quadrant they want to invest their time in, and then explain to them the power of Metcalf's Law, I believe you will have a person who is far more receptive to the business opportunity you are presenting. You may also want to explain the fact that network marketing is the fastest growing business model in the world today, even though they cannot see it because it is virtual or invisible.

Building a network marketing business is simply looking for friends, new and old, who want to go in the same direction you want to go. Just look at it as if solving a math problem. Let's say you bring 10 people, 10 new friends into the business. The value of your network is now worth 100, not 10. If those 10 people bring in 10 people each, the value of your business explodes. As I said at the start of this book, my mind was closed to network marketing when I first went to a business opportunity meeting in the early 1970s. I did not realize the power of the business opportunity sitting in front of me. Today I have seen the light. If I had to do it all over again, rather than build an old-style type of business, I would have started building a network marketing business.

A Better Idea That Costs Less To Get Into

Instead of building a network marketing business, I spent millions of dollars, and sometimes lost millions of dollars, building an old-style type of business. While I do not regret my journey of learning how to build an old-world type of business from scratch, I can now faithfully say to you that building a network marketing business makes more sense for most people—especially if you do not have millions of dollars to build an old-style type of business or hundreds of thousands of dollars to buy a famous franchise. Simply put, a network marketing business, with its low cost of entry and great training programs, is a far better idea—it is an idea whose time has come. The network marketing business is exploding worldwide. All you have to do is open your mind and you will see it. You cannot see it with your eyes because there is very little to see. There are no golden arches or green mermaids beckoning you to come into their place of business. The business of network marketing has exploded throughout the world and very few people can see it.

The Future Of Networking

Although the business has grown immensely, now is the time to get into the network marketing business. Why do I say that? I say that because the world has finally awakened to the idea that the Industrial Age is over and we are officially entering the Information Age. Big businesses such as General Electric and Ford Motor Company are Industrial Age businesses. Franchises such as McDonalds are transition businesses between the Industrial Age and the Information Age. Network marketing businesses are truly Information Age franchises simply because they run almost solely on information rather than on land, factories and employees.

When I was a kid my parents always said, "Go to school, and get good grades, so you can get a secure high-paying job with benefits." That is classic Industrial Age thinking. My parents truly believed in job security, a company pension and medical care as well as government Social Security and Medicare. Those are all old ideas from the Industrial Age. Today most of us know job security is a joke, and lifetime employment with one company is not a reality for most people. Then you add in retirement plans such as a 401(k), filled with risky stocks and mutual funds, the idea of retirement security is also a joke. Today, people need new ideas and systems where they can find the financial security our parents once had. One answer is network marketing. The more people wake up—and many are after the September 11th terrorist attack and the stock market crash—the more people will realize that network marketing is a new answer for a world with less and less security. Network marketing gives millions of people throughout the world the opportunity to take control of their lives and their financial future. That is why the network marketing industry will continue to grow, even though old-world thinkers fail to see it growing.

In Summary

Years ago when I was a young salesman trying to sell the first telecopiers— today known as fax machines—I had a lot of trouble selling the machines simply because so few people had one. As the numbers grew, the sale became easier and easier. The more fax machines there were, the more valuable the machine became. That is the power of Metcalf's Law.

Today the same struggles in selling the idea are true with network marketing. Years ago, many people laughed at network marketing. Many bad-mouthed the industry, giving it a bad name. I know I did. Today, with all the changes in the world, the future for the network marketing industry is only getting brighter. As stated earlier, many major corporations today have a network marketing division. Network marketing has finally become a mainstream business even though very few people realize it...yet. So even though your friends or co-workers cannot see the opportunity, all you have to do is open your mind and you will see the power of Metcalf's law. You will see the power of networks...the power that is right in front of you now. All you have to do is say, "I want the power of networks working for me."

The Next Value

In the next chapter, I will discuss the number-one business skill a person must have if they are to be successful in the real world of business. The beauty of network marketing is that it teaches you this very valuable skill you can use to increase your wealth for the rest of your life.

CHAPTER 7

Value #5: Developing Your Most Important Business Skill

The year 1974 was a turning point year in my life. I was being discharged from the U.S. Marine Corps and was about to enter the real world. My problem was which world was I going to enter? Was I going to enter the world of my poor dad and become an employee in the E quadrant, or was I going to enter the world of my rich dad and enter the world of the B quadrant?

As stated earlier, I had two professions with which I could have easily entered the E quadrant. I could have gone back to the shipping industry and become a ship's officer, sailing oil tankers for Standard Oil, or I could become a commercial airline pilot as many of my classmates did. Both professions were tempting, but I knew I did not want to be a ship's officer or a pilot for the rest of my life. Those days were behind me. Although it was a lot riskier and with fewer guarantees, I decided to follow in my rich dad's footsteps rather than my poor dad's.

In early 1974, before I was to be released from the Marine Corps, I went to my rich dad and asked him to train me for the world of the B quadrant. I still remember walking into his office in Waikiki and asking him for his advice for the next phase of my life. I was 26 years old and I knew I needed guidance in a world where very few people have gone, the world of the B quadrant. "What should I do?" I asked him. "What kind of training do I need?"

Looking up from his desk, without any hesitation, rich dad said, "Go get a job in sales."

"Sales?" I yelped like a dog that had been kicked. "I want to go into the B quadrant. I don't want to go into sales."

Rich dad stopped what he was doing, pulled off his glasses, gave me a stare from his uplifted eyes, and said, "You asked me what you should do next. I just told you what to do next. If you don't want to do what I recommend, get out of my office."

"But I want to become a business owner. I don't want to become a salesman." I argued back.

"Look," said rich dad. "How many times do I have to tell you that if you come looking for advice, then have the courtesy to listen to the advice I give you? If you don't want to listen to my advice, then don't ask for it. Got it?"

"So then explain to me, why sales?" I replied in a more humble tone. Both my dads were tough men, and I knew that if I was to learn something I had better listen with respect. "Tell me why learning how to sell is so important?"

> ## "The ability to sell is the number-one skill in business."

"The ability to sell is the number one skill in business," said rich dad. "The ability to sell is the most important skill of the B quadrant. If you cannot sell, don't bother thinking about becoming a business owner."

"The number-one skill?" I asked, repeating what he had said.

"The best salespeople are the best leaders," said rich dad. "Look at President Kennedy. He was one of the greatest speakers I have ever heard. When he spoke, people were inspired. That is because he had the power to speak to people's spirits."

"You mean when you're speaking from the stage or on television, that is selling too?" I asked.

"Of course," said rich dad. "And when you're writing, or speaking one-on-one, or speaking to your child, asking them to pick up their toys, that is all selling. Your high school teachers were trying to sell every day."

"Some didn't do a very good job," I replied with a smirk.

"Well, that is why they may not have been great teachers. All great teachers have been great salespeople. Look at Christ, Buddha, Mother Theresa, Gandhi, Mohammed. They were all great teachers, which means they were great salespeople."

"So the better I am at sales, the more successful in life I become?" I asked.

"And look at it the other way," replied rich dad. "Look at people who are the least successful in life. They are the people no one wants to listen to."

"Can anyone be good in sales?" I asked.

"Of course. We are all born sales people. Just watch a baby or young child. If they are hungry and aren't getting what they want, what do they do?"

"We are all born sales people."

"They start crying," I replied. "They communicate. They start selling."

"That's right," said rich dad. "Have you ever tried telling a child they can't have something? If the father won't give them what they want, they go to their mother. If their mother won't give them what they want, they get on the phone and call the grandparents. Somehow, as we grow older, some of us lose that 'I can have anything I want' attitude. As we grow older, we are told to stop asking for things. We are told to stop nagging, stop complaining, and stop being a pest. So we learn to stop selling."

"So as adults we have to *relearn* what we already knew," I said.

"Yes, if we want to be able to have what we want in our lives," said rich dad. "When I was about 30 years old, I realized I was falling behind in life. I was lacking something. I was working hard but things were not coming my way. Soon I realized that working harder and harder was not working. I finally accepted that if I did not make changes in me, I might end up with an empty life. Therefore, I knew I had to change myself. It slowly dawned on me that I did not know how to communicate with people. My employees did not listen to me. I would tell them to do something and they would either do something else or do nothing at all. My customers did not understand me. I would tell them why my products were better and they would still buy from someone else. I was awkward when talking to strangers. I was boring at parties. What I wanted to say wasn't being said. My communication skills were poor. It soon became obvious to me that if I wanted to be successful in business, I had to learn to sell. I needed to learn be a better communicator. I needed to come out of my shell. I had to learn to stop being afraid of people. I had to *relearn* what I once knew as a child." Rich dad paused for a while, his mind seeming to go back in time. Finally he looked up and said, "Do you remember a number of years ago, when both you and Mike were still in elementary school, I went to Honolulu to take a weeklong sales course?"

"I remember," I said. "My dad thought you were a fool for taking a course on selling."

"He did?" asked rich dad. "What did he say?"

"He said, 'Why would anyone spend so much money taking a course that you do not get college credit for?'"

With that, rich dad burst out laughing. "I spent my last $200 attending that course. However, that course has made me millions of dollars. And your dad was only thinking about college credits?"

"That's right," I said, cringing a little. "Different values. My dad wants more college degrees and you want more financial success."

Still chuckling, rich dad broke out his yellow legal tablet and wrote the following words:

Buy / Sell

Pointing to the words on the tablet rich dad said, "In business, these are two very important words. In the stock market and in real estate they are always talking about *buy/sell agreements.* A market as well as a business runs on buyers and sellers. If I had no buyers, I would be out of business. That means I've got to be continually selling. I sell to my employees, my investors, through advertising on TV and the newspaper, in my letters, and to my accountants and attorneys. All day long, I'm selling. I've got to keep my team moving forward and I have to keep happy customers coming in and going out even happier. So selling is more than trying to get somebody to give me some money."

"I understand that," I replied. "But why is learning to sell so important? Why is the ability to sell the number-one B quadrant skill?"

"Great question," said rich dad. "What most people fail to realize is that the more you can *sell,* the more you can *buy.*"

"What?" I asked, seeking greater clarity, knowing that I had just heard something very important. "The more I can sell the more I can buy?"

If You Want To Buy You Have To Sell Something First

Rich dad nodded, letting me think about what I was saying and learning. "You can only buy as much as you can sell," said rich dad. "If you want to buy something, you have to sell something first. That is why your ability to sell is the number one skill. You have to sell something first before you can buy something."

"So if I cannot sell, I cannot buy?" I asked.

Nodding, rich dad said, "Poor people are poor because they cannot sell, or they have nothing to sell. The same is true with poor nations. A poor nation is a nation with nothing to sell or a nation that cannot sell what it has. It is also true with people. There are many very talented people, but they cannot sell their talents. A business that cannot sell is out of business even if it has tons of inventory. When I find a business that is struggling financially, it is often because the leader of that business cannot sell. They may be smart, but they are simply poor communicators. I have met many middle managers that fail to climb the corporate ladder because they cannot sell. How many single lonely people have you met who cannot find the man or woman of their dreams simply because they fail to communicate what a good person they are?"

"You mean when I ask a girl out for a date, you consider that selling?"

"Very important selling," said rich dad. "The world is filled with many lonely people and poor people, simply because they were never taught how to sell, how to communicate, how to overcome their fear of rejection, or how to stand up again after being rejected?"

"So selling affects every aspect of life," I added.

"That is correct. That is why I spent my last dollar a number of years ago to take a course to learn how to sell. Today I have more money than your dad does because he has college credits and I have better selling skills. That is why I am saying to you that if you want to become a businessperson, learn how to sell, and keep improving your ability to sell. The better you are at selling, the richer you become."

Rich dad explained that his accountant sells his professional skills for a steady paycheck. He said, "When a person is applying for a job, he or she is in fact selling their professional services." He then added, "Everyone is selling something. When you go back to your house, everything you have there, the stove—the refrigerator, sofa, television, beds, everything—was sold to you. When you drive down the street, look at everything you see. Everything you have, someone sold it to you or you stole it. If you stole it, get out of my office because I do not do business with people who steal. I do business with people who sell."

"I did not realize selling was so important in business," I said. "I did not realize that if I wanted to be rich, I needed to learn how to sell."

"If you want to be successful in life, you need to learn how to sell," rich dad added. "Look at the real world. Politicians who win elections are great sales people. The most successful religious leaders are great sales people. The best teachers are the best sales people. Kids are born great sales people. Get my point?"

"I got it," I said. "But I am terrified of selling."

With that statement of truth, rich dad nodded and thought silently for a moment. "Thank you for your honesty," he said finally. "Most people are terrified of selling. Most people are terrified of rejection. Rather than admit their fear, they speak badly about sales people saying such things as, 'I'm not a sales person, I'm an educated professional.' "

"You mean most people lie about their fears," I said. "They pretend that the act of selling is below them."

"That's correct. So many people who are afraid of selling will not admit it. So they look down upon people who sell and the profession of sales," replied rich dad. "And the people who do that are often poor in one or two areas of their lives. Often they are poor in some personal success or in love. Most people who cannot sell are people who have to live below their means, shop at sales, or live frugally simply because they are afraid of selling. Their fear and lack of selling skills keeps them poor."

"But aren't most people afraid of rejection?" I asked.

> **"Successful people learn to overcome their fears rather than let their fears run their life."**

"Yes. Of course," said rich dad. "That is why successful people learn to overcome their fears rather than let their fears run their life. That is why I flew to Honolulu with my last few dollars to take a sales course. That is why I give you the same advice I gave myself. My advice is to go learn to sell. I'll say it again: When someone is poor, unsuccessful, or lonely, it is because he or she has failed to sell something. If you want to get what you want, you have to sell something first."

"So I can buy anything I want if I can sell?" I added.

Rich dad nodded. "That is why selling is your most important skill. Are you ready to learn how to sell?"

My Sales Education Begins

After that talk, I took rich dad's advice and was soon applying to both IBM and Xerox for a job. I applied to those two companies not for their compensation plan, but for their sales training. Many network marketing companies also provide excellent training programs for their people. To me, learning to sell and overcome my fear of rejection and get my point across is the best education I have ever received. Learning to sell changed my life. Learning to sell changed my future.

Bringing Out The Winner In You

There is more to sales training than learning to sell. When I first started out with Xerox, I was extremely shy. Even though I had great training with Xerox, my fears still prevented me from knocking on doors or getting on the phone. I still have the same fears today. The difference is I eventually gained the self-confidence to overcome my personal fears and make that phone call or knock on the door. If I had not learned how to get over my own personal fears, the loser inside of me would have won. Rich dad often said, "There is a *rich person* and a *poor person* inside each of us. There is also a *winner* and a *loser* inside of each of us. Every time we let our fears, our doubts, or our low self-esteem win, the loser wins. Learning to sell is learning to overcome the loser inside of you. Learning to sell also brings out the winner in you."

> **"Learning to sell is learning to overcome the loser inside of you. Learning to sell also brings out the winner in you."**

One of the beauties of network marketing is that it gives you the opportunity to face your fears, deal with them, overcome them, and let the winner in you win. The beauty of network marketing companies is that the leaders in the organization have the patience to work with you while you are learning. In the real world of business, if you cannot sell in three to six months, you are fired. Xerox was a little more generous. They gave me a year to learn and a year of probation. If I did not have the two years, I know I would have been fired. Finally, just before being fired, my self-confidence began to grow, my sales improved, and two years later, I was consistently number one or number two in my office. Increasing my self-esteem was more important than my paycheck. Rebuilding my self-confidence and my self-esteem has been priceless. And it has helped me earn millions of dollars. For that, I will always be grateful to the Xerox Corporation and the staff that taught me how to sell, and more importantly, to overcome my demons, doubts and fears. Today, I strongly recommend network marketing because the industry offers the same opportunity to strengthen and rebuild your self-confidence that the Xerox Corporation offered me.

Sales Training Helped Me Meet The Woman Of My Dreams

On a side note, without my sales skills and, more importantly, my self-confidence, I doubt if I would have met and married the woman of my dreams. When I first met my wife Kim, I thought she was the most beautiful woman in the world. Today, I find her even more beautiful because she is beautiful on the outside but even more beautiful on the inside.

When I first saw her, I was speechless. I was afraid to walk up to her. However, the sales training on how to overcome my fears was going to pay off. Instead of hiding in the back of the room, stuffing my face at the chip and dip table, staring at her from afar and not talking to her (which I used to do whenever I saw a woman I was attracted to) I walked boldly forward and said, "Hi." My sales training was paying off.

Kim turned, smiled her beautiful smile, and I was in love. She was friendly, charming and we could talk about anything. We just seemed to get along. She was right out of my dreams. However, when I asked her out, she said, "No." Being a good salesman, I asked her out again and again she said, "No." Even though my self-confidence was bruised and my male ego was fading, I asked her out again. Again the answer was, "No." This went on for six months. For six months, she said, "No." If I had not learned how to overcome the self-doubts about myself, I could never have kept asking for six months. I was hurting inside. Each time she said, "No," I went into hiding to lick my wounded ego. After six months of being rejected, my fragile male ego was deflated, yet I kept asking. Finally, one day, she said, "Yes," and we have been together ever since.

While we were dating, many of my male friends kept saying, "I can't believe she goes out with you. She's a fox and you're a dog. You look like the beauty and the beast." Silently I could hear my rich dad saying, "Selling is the most important skill in business. It is also your most important skill in life."

You can see a picture of Kim and me on the back of the book, *Retire Young Retire Rich*. It is a picture of Kim and me on an island in Fiji on horseback, smiling from ear to ear, because that was the day we celebrated becoming financially free. In my heart, I know I would not have made it in life without Kim. She is the woman of my dreams and she has made my life complete. This year, 2004, we celebrate 18 years of marriage.

A Word On Rejection

The other day I heard a commercial on the radio saying, "It's a great business. There is no selling." I thought to myself, "What kind of person would be attracted to a job, much less a business, without selling?" I then realized that most people are attracted to a job without selling, even though we all sell something. The more I thought about it, the more I realized that most people aren't against selling they just dislike rejection. I know I do. I hate being rejected. Since most people hate rejection, I thought I would add a different point of view on the word *rejection*.

Over twenty years ago when I was a struggling sales rep for Xerox, I went to my rich dad and told him I hated rejection. I said, "More than hating rejection, I live in fear of rejection. I find myself doing everything possible to avoid any situation where I might be rejected. I sometimes think I would rather die than be rejected. Every time I knocked on a door and a secretary said, 'We already have a copier,' or, 'We are not interested in a new copier, especially one from Xerox,' or, 'The boss does not talk to salesmen,' or, 'We like your proposal, but we are going with your competitor IBM,' I wanted to crawl into a hole and die. The more I thought about being rejected, the more I want to quit selling and run away. The more I run away from rejection, the more my boss at Xerox says he is going to fire me."

Rejection = Success

For me, my fear of rejection, low self-esteem and lack of self-confidence was ruining my life. On the surface, I appeared confident and outgoing. I came across as John Wayne the U.S. Marine on the outside, yet truthfully, on the inside, I was Pee Wee Herman. It was at this low point in my life, just before I was to be fired, that rich dad handed down some of his best words of wisdom for me. On the day I was put on probation by my sales manager at

Xerox, rich dad said to me, "The most successful people in the world are the most rejected people in the world."

"What?" I asked, not sure if I heard the right thing. "The most successful people in the world are the most rejected?"

"You heard me," said rich dad. "And on the flip side, the people who are the least rejected are the least successful."

"So if I want to be successful in life, I need to be rejected more and more," I said.

"You got it," smiled rich dad.

"I don't understand. Please explain." I asked.

"Look at the President of the United States. Forty-nine percent of the voters—tens of millions of them—voted against him. They rejected him. Have you ever had millions of people reject you?"

"No," I said.

"Well, when you do, you will be famous and successful."

"But he also had millions of people accept him," I added.

"That is true," said rich dad. "But could he ever have become President of the United States if he was afraid of rejection?"

"No, I guess not. I know there are many people who more than reject him. Many people hate him. He has to have guards around him because people want to kill him. I don't think I could take that kind of pressure."

"And that may be why you may not attain the kind of success you want or are capable of. The point is no one likes being rejected. Yet the lesson of the day is the people who run from rejection are the least successful people on the planet. That does not mean they are not nice people; it just means they are not as successful as people who are rejected a lot...people who do not run from rejection."

"So if I want to become successful in life, I need to risk being more and more rejected?" I asked.

"That is correct," said rich dad. "Look at the Pope. He is a great man and a great religious leader and yet he is greatly rejected. Millions of people do not like what he says or what he stands for."

"That means rather than act like a wimp and let my sales manager fire me, I should go out and start getting rejected."

"Well if you don't start getting rejected, you definitely will get fired." Rich dad smiled. "Look, don't be a fool and run out into the world and splatter your face up against the walls of life. Yes, you do need to risk being rejected, but you must also learn from your rejection, and that means correction."

"Rejection and correction," I said.

Nodding, rich dad wrote out the formula he learned from his sales training years before in Honolulu, the training for which he paid $200.

Rejection and Correction = Education and Acceleration

"I have followed this formula for years. Each time I am rejected, I ask myself, 'What did I do wrong? What could I have done better?' If I don't come up with a good answer, I'd then talk to someone about the sales call, review what happened, maybe role-play, and repeat the situation where my friend is the buyer and I am the seller. The point is I don't call the person who rejected me a 'jerk,' 'bum,' 'cheap skate,' or 'loser.' I suspend such nonsense and mentally thank the person for giving me an opportunity to learn, correct, and improve myself.' I ask myself, 'Next time, how could I have handled the situation differently and better.'"

"And that leads to your *education* and your *acceleration* in life," I added.

"In my opinion, it is the formula for success for anything in life," said rich dad.

"But if I avoid rejection, the process does not begin?" I asked. "Rejection is the start of education."

Nodding, rich dad smiled and said, "You've got it. That is why people who avoid rejection are, in the long run, less successful in life than those who face rejection. Most people are not successful because they have not been rejected enough."

> **"The more I risk being *rejected*, the better my chances are of being *accepted*."**

"I got it," I said with a smile to rich dad. A few days later, I volunteered to work for a non-profit charity dialing for dollars on their phone team. I wasn't doing it for the money. I was doing it so I could help a worthy cause and to get rejected more. I realized that working for Xerox, my rejections per day were too few. By dialing for dollars at night, I could get the number of rejections up. I knew the more I was rejected, the more I could correct. The more I corrected, the more educated I became. And the more educated I became, the more successful I became. Three nights a week, after work at Xerox, I worked at the office of this charity. For a year, I dialed for dollars for free. In that year, I went from nearly being fired from Xerox to becoming their number-one salesperson for the next two years. Once I had achieved sales success at Xerox, I resigned and went full-time into my then part-time nylon and Velcro surfer wallet business. I was beginning my journey into the B quadrant. The lesson I learned was that the more I risk being *rejected*, the better my chances are of being *accepted*.

98 Percent Rejection

Before moving on from this subject of rejection, I thought it best to offer you some real-world realities on the subject. When I was temporarily in business school, one of the professors said, "To be successful in business, you need to be right at least 51 percent of the time." In my opinion, that is inaccurate information. In reality, a person can be very successful with a much lower percentage of success.

For example, in the direct mail business, if a company mails out 1 million pieces of mail and gets back a 2 percent response, that is often considered very successful. What that really means is that 98 percent of the people said, "No." Ninety-eight percent rejected the mailing and that is still 2,000 who say, "Yes." In fact, for most mass-market campaigns, a 98 percent rejection is considered great.

The lesson for you is this: if you want to become more successful in life, simply seek more rejection and then correction. The beauty of a network marketing business is that the leaders encourage you to go out and get some rejection. What an opportunity. If you truly desire greater success in life, join a network marketing company and learn to overcome your fears of rejection. If you spend five years doing that, I bet that the rest of your life would be vastly more successful. At least it has been for me. In fact, I continue to seek more and more opportunities for rejection. That is why I learned to be a public speaker and go on television with my infomercials. Today, millions of people all over the world are rejecting me. That is why I am getting richer and richer.

Teaching Versus Selling

Network marketing offers greater challenges than Xerox did for me. The reason I say that is because at Xerox, all I had to do was learn to sell. In network marketing, not only do you have to learn to sell; you also have to learn to teach others to sell. If you can sell, but you cannot teach others to sell, you will not be successful in network marketing. That means the great thing about network marketing is that if you are going to be successful, you have to be a great teacher. If you love teaching, you will do well in network marketing.

Personally, teaching is far more rewarding than just selling. The beauty of a network marketing business is that the business trains you to be a teacher, not just a salesperson. If you love learning and teaching a network marketing business is a great business to join. That is why I titled this book, *The Business School For People Who Like Helping People.*

Sales Managers Don't Sell; They Teach

While I was doing my market research on the different network marketing businesses, I found many successful people who worked very hard and could sell, but they were not successful with their business. The reason they were not successful is that they were selling for those who could not sell. For example, I went to this meeting and a new business owner had invited several of his friends and family to come learn about the business opportunity. As I sat in the room listening to the presentation, I realized that the new business owner's *upline sponsor* did the entire presentation. The new business owner said nothing.

After the meeting, I asked the new business owner if his upline leader spent any time teaching him the nuts and bolts of selling. He said, "No. My upline just wants us to get people to the meeting. He's the only one who does the selling because he is the best salesperson."

Right there I knew there was a flaw in this particular network marketing company's educational system. First, the training was a joke. This company had a reading list but no one ever read any of the books. Secondly, it only wanted people starting businesses to bring their friends and family so the better salespeople could sell them. It was not a business school. It was a sales school.

While I was at Xerox, my sales manager, Charlie Robinson was one of the best teachers I have ever had. I would make the appointments and Charlie would go along on the sales call with me. During the call, he said very little. After the call, we would go back to his office and we would analyze the sales presentation. We would then discuss my strong and weak points. After the lessons and corrections, Charlie would then run several sales training drills and exercises to strengthen my sales skills, especially the skill of overcoming rejection. That is how I became a sales person. I became a sales person because I had a great teacher. Although a great salesman himself, once Charlie became a sales manager, he had to become a teacher. And a great teacher he was. That is why he sat silently on most of my sales calls. Occasionally he would step in to show me what to do, but most of the time, he sat silently letting me make my mistakes. The message is to be successful in network marketing, you have to be like Charlie Robinson: a great sales person and a great teacher. Once you learn to do that, the business becomes a dream come true.

Sales Dogs

My dear friend of over 20 years, Blair Singer, a Rich Dad's Advisor and author of *Sales Dogs* and *The ABC's of Building a Business Team That Wins,* and I have been selling for years. We both started out in Hawaii as junior sales representatives. He joined the Burroughs Corporation, today known as UNISYS, about the same time I joined the Xerox Corporation. We went through the world of corporate sales training. One thing that Blair and I have observed is that many network marketing business owners may learn to sell, but they fail because they fail to become great sales managers. In the world of corporate America, sales managers are teachers, not just sales people.

In his book *Sales Dogs,* Blair discusses the different types of sales people found in any sales organization and how each dog needs to be trained differently. Blair says, "The reason sales training is so important in a network marketing business is because not only do you have to learn how to sell; you also have to learn how to teach others to sell. If you do not teach others to sell, you will not be successful in a network marketing business."

Credit Card Debt

One of the reasons so many people are in credit card debt today is because they cannot sell. When people buy things on credit, they are in reality selling their future labor. In many cases, when credit cards are used, people are selling their *tomorrows* in order to buy something *today.* The reason most people are in credit card debt is that they have been taught to be great *buyers,* but not to be great *sellers.*

Rather than sell your *tomorrows,* I recommend joining a network marketing business and learn how to sell. If you learn to sell and build a successful network marketing business, you will be able to use your credit card to buy what you want and pay the credit card bill off at the end of each month. To me that makes more sense than selling your *tomorrows.* You and I know that there is not much of a future when you sell your *tomorrows.*

In Summary

Simply said, the ability to sell is a very important life skill for everyone. Even my cat sells. In fact, my cat is better at sales than most people are. Every morning, if I do not feed her when she's hungry, that little cat will let me know what she wants and when she wants it. Humans are trained not to do that. A network marketing business can restore your natural ability to get what you want in life by teaching you how to sell and teaching you how to teach others how to sell.

The Next Value

In the next chapter, we will go into how a network marketing business helps you develop your leadership skills. My rich dad said, "In the B quadrant, leadership skills are not optional."

CHAPTER 8

Value #6: Leadership

Both my rich dad and my poor dad were great leaders. My real dad was the head of education for the State of Hawaii. He was a great speaker and he worked diligently to improve the quality of education for children in the state. My rich dad was also a great leader. He inspired his workers and his investors to help him build a great business empire. When I returned from Vietnam, my rich dad reminded me of the importance of working to develop my leadership skills. He said, "Leaders do what most people are afraid of doing." That may be why there are so few business leaders in the B quadrant. In this chapter, I will discuss the value of the leadership skills a person develops in a network marketing business.

One of the reasons my rich dad encouraged me to go into the Marine Corps, and then on to Vietnam, was to develop my leadership skills. In Vietnam, I discovered that great leaders were not tough people who yelled and screamed or were physically abusive. In the heat of battle, I found that great leaders were often quiet, brave, and when they spoke, they spoke to our souls and our spirits. One of great values of a network business is that it helps build that kind of leadership skill in their leaders.

Leadership Skills Are Not Optional

My rich dad would also say, "There are leaders found in every quadrant. However, you do not have to be a leader to be successful in every quadrant…except for the B quadrant. In the B quadrant, leadership skills are not optional." He would continue, "Money does not go to the business with the best products or service. Money flows to the business with the best leaders and the best management team."

If you look at the CASHFLOW Quadrant, there are leaders found in each quadrant.

My poor dad, for instance, was a dynamic leader in the E quadrant while my rich dad was a leader in the B and I quadrants. From a very early age, both dads stressed the importance of developing my leadership skills. That is why both dads recommended I join the Boy Scouts, play sports, and go into the military. When I look back on what training best supported my professional and financial success, I would say it was not the subjects I studied in school, but the training I received in scouting, sports and the military.

In 1974, as I drove off the Marine Corps Air Station for the last time, leaving the world of the military and entering the world of business. I remember asking myself, "I wonder if my leadership skills will be good enough?" Those of you who know what happened to me after leaving the military already know that the leadership training I received in the scouts, sports and the military was not enough for the challenges of the B quadrant business world that awaited me. I had a lot more to learn.

The reason my military leadership skills were inadequate is simply because the rules, the context and the environments are different between the military and the business world. When preparing for war, we knew that if we were poor leaders, people died. In the world of business, if you are a poor leader, you are sued or someone files a complaint with his or her union representative. In the military we were motivated by the fear of dying, the value of our team, and the importance of our mission. In the civilian world, I often found exact opposite values of motivation. In the world of business, it was *security,* not *freedom,* that motivated people, *money* not *mission, individual* not *team,* and *management* not *leadership.* It is due to these differences in values that I had a tough time in the world of business and continue to struggle with the differences today.

Oh, I know that when an employee goes to the company rally, the managers talk about the company mission, the importance of team spirit, and all those lofty ideals. Yet, in most businesses today, I have found the money, benefits and security are the real glue. When I began looking at different network marketing companies, I began to find many leaders—again, not all of them—who had the same core values I found in military leaders. They valued the importance of the mission, the team, and freedom. Most of the leaders in the networking business I met, young or old, were truly inspiring. They were not like most of the managers I found in the corporate world who thought they were leaders.

Managers Are Not Leaders

To me, one of the biggest values of a network marketing business is the leadership training you receive that gives you the education, the time, and the opportunities to develop one of your most important business skills essential for success in the B quadrant. Those leadership skills are very different from the management skills most often required for the E and S quadrants. Now don't get me wrong. Management skills are very important skills, but one must know the difference between management skills and leadership skills, whether you have developed them, and when to use them. As my rich dad would say, "Managers are not necessarily leaders and leaders are not necessarily managers."

Whenever I meet someone from the E or S quadrant having difficulties making the transition to the B quadrant, I often find someone with great technical or management skills, but with little leadership ability. For example, a friend of a friend came to me because he wanted to raise some money to start his own restaurant. He is a brilliant and well-trained chef with many years of fine dining experience. He had a unique new concept for his restaurant, a well-written business plan, great financial projections, a great location already selected, and a clientele that would follow him to his new restaurant. All he needed was someone to invest $500,000.

It has been five years since he wrote his business plan. It is a great plan, but everyone he has asked to invest in his business plan, including me, has turned him down. Today, he is still working in the same restaurant as an employee; he is still a great chef; and he is still looking for the $500,000 in start-up capital. I do not know why the other investors did not invest with him, but I can tell you why I did not invest. The following are the reasons I did not invest:

Reason #1: Although he had experience, charm, and charisma, he lacked the leadership skills to inspire confidence. Although he could start a restaurant and run it successfully, I doubted if he could make it a big restaurant chain. His lack of confidence said, "I'll be successful, but I will always be small." In other words, he has great *management* skills, but I doubt if he has the *leadership* skills required to make his plan work. I do not doubt that he could manage 10 restaurants, but I doubt if he has the leadership skills to build a business that built 10 restaurants. He needs a business partner with the leadership skills and the business skills, but being a typical person moving from the E to the S quadrant, he does not want partners. He wants to build his dream business on his own.

Reason #2: When you look at the CASHFLOW Quadrant, the difference between the S and B quadrants is size. For example, if you heard someone say, "I want to open a hamburger stand on corner of 6th Street and Vine Street," you would know that this person would most likely be stuck in the S quadrant for a long time. Now if you heard someone else say, "I want to open a hamburger stand on every major street corner in every major city throughout the world, and I will call this business McDonalds," you would instantly know that this person plans to open the same hamburger stand, but this person plans to build a business in the B quadrant. In other words, it is the same hamburger business, but from different quadrants. My rich dad would have said, "The difference in the number of street corners is the difference of leadership."

Therefore, I did not invest because I doubt if I would have ever gotten my investment back. It wasn't because the business would fail, but I doubted that I would get my money back because he would have probably always remained small, though successful. In addition, if he did pay it back, it might take a long time to get it back. If you ask most professional investors, they are not interested in how good a restaurant is. They want to know how big the restaurant chain will grow.

Reason #3: The third reason I did not invest is that if he was to remain small, then why should I invest? I would be excited to invest if he was going to be big, and possibly turn my $500,000 into tens of millions of dollars. By lacking the leadership skills to make the restaurant big, it was doubtful that he could turn my $500,000 into millions of dollars. That is the price of lacking the leadership skills to take a business from the S quadrant into the B quadrant. As my rich dad said, "Money does not go to the business with the best products or service. Money flows to the business with the best leaders and management teams."

Reason #4: The fourth reason for not investing with him was because he had to be the smartest member on his team. He had an ego problem. As my rich dad often said, "If you're the leader of the team and you're also the smartest person on the team, your team is in trouble." What my rich dad meant was that in many S quadrant businesses the head of the business is often the smartest person. For example, you go to see the doctor or dentist—not the receptionist—for your medical and dental needs.

In a B quadrant business, leadership skills are important simply because the B person has to deal with people who are much smarter, more experienced, and more capable than he is or she is. For example, I saw my rich dad—a man without any formal education—deal with bankers, lawyers, accountants, investment advisors, etc., in order to do his job. Most of them had master's degrees and some doctorate degrees. In other words, to do his job, he had to lead and direct people who were far more educated and educated in many different professional fields. In order to raise money for his business, he often had to deal with people who were far richer than he was.

"A" Students Work For "C" Students

In many cases, an S quadrant person deals only with clients, peers, such as other doctors and lawyers, and subordinates. In order to make the switch to the B quadrant, a quantum leap in leadership skills, not technical skills, is often required. In other words, if you have great leadership skills, you can afford to hire smart technical people a business needs to grow, people such as lawyers, accountants, CEOs, presidents, vice-presidents, engineers and managers. As I stated in earlier books, the "A "students work for the "C" students, and the "B" students work for the government. If you are a "C" student, and "C" stands for *communicator,* and you have great leadership skills, you can afford to hire the "A" students who have great technical skills.

Leadership Is Not Optional

One day this same friend of a friend called to ask me why I did not invest in his restaurant. I more or less told him the four reasons discussed above. Hurt and defensive, he said, "But I have the best training in the world. Chefs from all over the world dream of attending the culinary school I attended. I have years of experience not only in the kitchen but also in managing the restaurant. How can you say I lack leadership skills?"

> **"In growing a business, leadership skills are a necessity."**

After a bit of patient explaining, saying to him that money, confidence and leadership go hand in hand, he began to understand my point. Yet, I think he still missed a lot. Finally, he said, "But why do I need leadership skills when I have such a great education and years of experience?" When I recommended that he join a network marketing company that taught business education as well as leadership development, he got angry and said, "I am in the restaurant business. I do not need any more business education and leadership development." I realized that to him, lifelong business education and continuing leadership development were optional. To my rich dad, growing business leadership skills are a necessity. To him, leadership skills are not optional in the B quadrant.

The Best Training In The World

As I stated at the start of this book, one of the most important values I found in some network marketing businesses was their life-changing business education. I also found some of the best business and leadership development programs in the world. To me the value of those programs is priceless for those who want to move from the E and S quadrants, into the B quadrant.

Since doing my research, and dropping my prejudices against the industry, I have met many successful entrepreneurs who received their business education in a network marketing business. Recently I met a young man who made hundreds of millions of dollars from his computer business. He said to me, "I was just a young computer programmer for years. One day a friend took me to a meeting and I signed up in his network marketing business. For six years, all I did was go to meetings, attend events, read books and listen to tapes. Today I have hundreds of tapes and piles of books in my closet from those days. Not only did I eventually become successful in the network marketing business, but I also used what I learned to quit my programming job once the income from my network marketing business provided me enough residual income to start my own computer business. Three years ago, I took my computer business public and made over $48 million net after tax profit. I could not have done that without the training I got from that network marketing company. It was the best business and leadership development training in the world."

Leaders Speak To Your Spirit

In doing my research, I went to many meetings and large events. At the events, I heard some of the best business leaders speaking to inspire others to find their own personal greatness. As I heard many of these individuals tell their stories of starting with nothing and eventually becoming wealthy beyond their wildest dreams, I realized that the business was doing the same thing my rich dad told me to do: to become a leader. While they seemed to be talking a lot about money, they were really inspiring people to get out of their shells, go beyond their fears, and go for their dreams that make life worth living. To do that required leadership skills on the part of the speaker. The reason it takes leadership is because many people use the same types of words about *dreams, more time with family,* and *freedom.* But few people are inspired enough to trust and follow the speaker of these overused words.

Killing Your Spirit

Earlier in this book, this diagram was used in the chapter on the value of life-changing education. That chapter talked about the power of education needing to influence more than just your thoughts. Life changing education affects you mentally, emotionally, spiritually and physically. The following is a diagram of someone using emotion to motivate a person into doing something physically.

Communicating Emotion-To-Emotion

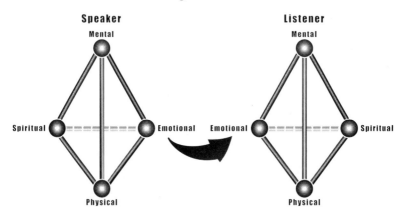

School for me used many mental tricks to frighten me emotionally into studying hard and getting good grades. As I grew up, I also found many people who could motivate you using different types of emotional ploys in order to get you to do something they wanted you to do.

The following are examples of a person using some type of emotional ploy in their communication:

1. "If you don't get good grades, you won't get a good job."
2. "If you don't come to work on time, you'll be fired."
3. "If you elect me, I will make sure you don't lose your Social Security benefits."
4. "Play it safe. Don't take unnecessary risks."
5. "Join my business. You can make a lot of money."
6. "Let me show you how to get rich quick."
7. "Do as I tell you."

8. "As you know, the company is having a rough time. If you don't want to get fired, you'd best not ask for a raise."

9. "You can't afford to quit. Who will pay you as much as I do?"

10. "You've only got eight more years to retirement. Don't make any waves."

In my opinion, too much of communication today uses fear or greed to motivate people into doing something. When the emotions of fear and greed are the primary motivators, it kills our spirits.

True Leaders Inspire The Spirit

When I was in Vietnam, there was a lot of emotionally-based communication. Yet what ultimately made some of our leaders great was that they could speak to our spirits. They could speak beyond our fears of dying and speak directly to our souls, that part of us that is powerful and invincible. The following are words spoken by great leaders. These words go beyond our doubts and fears and speak to our spirits, as the diagram below depicts:

Communicating Spirit-To-Spirit

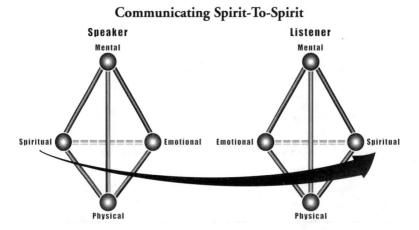

You may remember some of these words that touched our souls and many are recorded in history.

1. "The time is near at hand which must determine whether Americans are to be free or to be slaves." —*George Washington*

2. "Give me liberty or give me death." —*Patrick Henry*

3. "Remember the Alamo." —*A Texas battle cry*

4. "Four score and seven years ago." And also, "Am I not destroying my enemies when I make friends of them?" —*Abraham Lincoln*

5. "You can't hold a man down without staying down with him." —*Booker T. Washington*

6. "Ask not what your country can do for you… " —*John F. Kennedy*
7. "I have a dream…" —*Martin Luther King*
8. "Winning is a habit. Unfortunately, so is losing." —*Vince Lombardi*
9. "Only our individual faith in freedom can keep us free." —*Dwight Eisenhower*
10. "Cowards can never be moral." —*Gandhi*
11. "Don't be humble; you're not that great." —*Golda Meir*
12. "Being powerful is like being a lady. If you have to tell people you are, you aren't." —*Margaret Thatcher*
13. "Do not let what you cannot do interfere with what you can do." —*John Wooden*
14. "My best friend is the one who brings out the best in me." —*Henry Ford*
15. "Try not to become a man of success, but rather try to become a man of value." —*Albert Einstein*

In Summary: Three Different Types Of Leaders

The beauty of a network marketing leadership program is that it brings out a different type of leader. The military developed a type of leader that inspired men and women to defend their country. The world of business develops a type of leader that builds teams to beat the competition. In the network marketing world, the type of leader that is developed is a leader that influences others by being a great teacher, teaching others to fulfill their life's dreams by teaching others to go for their dreams. Instead of beating the enemy or beating the competition, most network marketing leaders simply inspire and teach others to find the financial bounty this world offers without harm to others.

In summary, all three types of leadership speak to the human spirit, but the different leadership styles bring out a different type of leader. If you love to lead by teaching, by influencing and inspiring others to find their own world of financial abundance without having to beat the competition, then a network marketing business may be right for you.

The Next Value

The next chapter is about the difference in value between *money* and *wealth*. Unfortunately, most people have been trained to work for money when instead they should be working to build wealth. One of the reasons many people are not successful in a network marketing business is because they come to the business looking for money rather than looking for an opportunity to build wealth. As rich dad said, "The rich don't work for money. The poor and middle class do that."

CHAPTER 9

Value # 7: Not Working For Money

On a talk radio program in 2002, a caller asked me this question:

"I am an electrical engineer who works for a large Silicon Valley computer company. As you know, the high-tech industry has been devastated, especially here in California. I have not been fired but I have been asked to take a cut in pay and work fewer hours. You know how expensive real estate has been here in the Bay Area. My mortgage payment is almost as much as my reduced paycheck. I am afraid I might lose my house if I have to take another pay cut. On top of that, my retirement plan, my 401(k), has been nearly wiped out. What should I do?"

"Have you tried selling your house?" was my first question.

"I have," said the caller. *"The problem is the value of the house has gone down so far that I owe more than the house is worth. If I were to sell it, I would have to pay the buyer money rather than them paying me money. Then I still have the same problem of where to live. Rents are as high as mortgage payments."*

"What does your wife do?" I asked.

"She works for a child care center. They're having trouble too because so many families have moved out of the area. Her job is secure but they don't pay her much."

"Why doesn't she look for a higher paying job?" I asked.

"She'd like to but one of the benefits of working at the child care center is that our two children get to go there for free. If she had to pay for child care, the child care would be almost as much as her salary at another company."

"Have you considered starting a part-time home-based business?" I asked.

"I told you we don't have any money left. How can I start a business without any money?"

"Have you and your wife looked into starting a network marketing business at home? They don't require much money to get started and they will train you." I asked.

"Oh yeah, we looked into those scams. They don't pay anything. They expect us to work for two to three years before we can make any money. We need money today, not two to three years from now."

The host of the radio program interrupted to let us know his program was out of time and the program ended. The caller and I never had a chance to complete our dialogue.

The reason I mention this broadcast interview is that it illustrates the difference in core values. The caller obviously is in need of money and I do empathize. As some of you know, my wife and I have been flat broke, even homeless for a few weeks…so I do know how it feels to need money.

Yet the reason Kim and I were able to become financially free in fewer than 10 years was simply because we knew the difference between *money* and *wealth*. If you would like to know more about how Kim and I went from nothing to financially free in fewer than 10 years, that story is told in the Rich Dad book, *Rich Dad's Retire Young Retire Rich*. In addition, the Rich Dad book, *Rich Dad's CASHFLOW Quadrant,* begins with Kim and me being homeless in 1985, the worst year of our lives. I mention those two books for those of you who may question my understanding of how it feels to be broke and busted. Both books go into how we got out of our financial mess. Let me assure you that Kim and I know what it feels like to have nothing and that is why we prefer to be rich and financially free. To us, not having enough money to live on was a horrible way to live. It hurt us more than financially. Being out of money tested our marriage, our self-confidence, and our self-worth.

Three Ways To Live

Long after that radio program was over, the feeling that I was left with after the phone call with the young father ended disturbed me. As stated in the previous chapter, we can speak to each other spirit-to-spirit or emotion-to-emotion. In this case, our communication wavelength was the emotion of fear. I could feel his fear and it hurt for me to feel it. I knew exactly how that fear feels.

The value described in this chapter is really about feelings. Kim and I personally know that when it comes to money, there are three feelings and three different ways to live with those feelings:

1. The feeling of fear. When Kim and I were homeless and without money, the feeling of fear was paralyzing. It was so intense that it numbed our entire bodies. That was the feeling I was receiving over the phone with the young father. It was also the same feeling I had as a young child, growing up in my family. My mom and dad were poor and out of money for most of their marriage. The feeling of not having enough money hung over our family for most of my childhood.

2. The feeling of anger and frustration. The second way of living is living with the emotion of anger or frustration from having to get up and go to work, especially when you would rather be doing something else. A person who lives with this feeling may be someone who has a good job and high pay, but they cannot afford to stop working. That is where the frustration comes from. They know if they stop, the world they live in would come crashing down. People like this may say, "I cannot afford to quit. If I quit, the banks would come and take everything away." These people often say, "I can't wait until my next vacation," or "Only 10 more years to retirement."

3. The feeling of joy, peace and contentment. The third way of living is to live with the peace of mind of knowing that regardless of whether you work or not, there is plenty of money coming in. Ever since 1994, when Kim and I sold our business and retired, this is the feeling we have lived. Kim was 37 and I was 47. To me it is a feeling, a way of life that is worth working toward. While we still work today, the feeling of not having to work, to be able to quit anytime, and still have more than enough money coming in for as long as we live is a great feeling.

The Difference Between Money And Wealth

What I wanted to say to that young father during the radio interview was that his problems would not go away if he continued to work for money. When I suggested to him that he start a network marketing business, part-time and with his wife, it was that it might be time for them to start working to acquire wealth rather than a bigger paycheck. When he said, "Oh yeah, we looked into those scams. They don't pay anything. They expect us to work for two to three years before we can make any money. We need money today, not two to three years from now." I knew that in order for the quality of his life to change, he would need to change his values. In other words, I had no doubt that he and his wife would ultimately find more money and that they would find a new life. I suspect that if they did not change their core values, they would remain for the rest of their lives in Life #2, living with anger and frustration all their lives simply because they chose to work for money rather than wealth.

What Is Wealth?

In previous books and other rich dad products, I mention that wealth is not measured in money; instead, wealth is measured in time. Our definition is:

Wealth is the ability to survive so many number of days forward.

As I said, wealth is measured in time. For example, if all I have to my name is $1,000 in savings and my living expenses are $100 a day, then my wealth is 10 days. If my living expenses are $50 then my wealth is 20 days. That is an overly simplified example explaining this definition of wealth; and again, wealth is measured in *time* rather than money. Health and wealth are similar because both are measured in time. We have all heard stories of a doctor saying to someone, "You have six months to live." The doctor is giving the patient an assessment of his or her health as measured in time. I know a person who is so far behind financially that he measures his wealth saying, "I am negative two months wealthy." In other words, he is truly living on borrowed time and borrowed money.

It has been said that the average American family is less than three paychecks away from financial disaster. If the average pay period is two weeks, or 14 days, that means, the average American family is 44 days wealthy. After that, their standard of living goes down. That is the problem with working for money rather than for wealth.

Before moving on, you may want to ask yourself this question: "If I (and if married, your spouse and you) stop working today, how long could I survive financially?" Your answer is your wealth today. The good news is that your wealth can be greatly increased even if you do not make much money today.

Network Marketing Teaches You To Work For Wealth

During my period of researching the different network marketing companies, one of the hardest value points the speakers had to explain was the difference between working for money and working for wealth.

In one of the opportunity meetings I went to, a guest raised his hand and asked, "How much money will I earn?" Unfortunately, the person leading the meeting did not do an adequate job explaining to the group the difference between building a business and working at a job. More importantly, he didn't explain the difference between money and wealth. I am afraid that most people left puzzled or frustrated at the answers they got.

One answer the speaker gave was, "Your income is unlimited." The problem with that answer is that most people attending the meeting were not looking for unlimited wealth, but for the opportunity to make an extra $1,000 to $3,000 a month. In my opinion, they are still thinking in terms of money rather than wealth. In other words, there are two kinds of money. One is money that comes from labor and the other is money that comes from assets. If you want to become wealthy, you need money that comes from assets. If you want to work hard all your life, then just work for money, which is what most people do.

The next point of confusion came when the speaker said, "OK, if all you want is an extra $3,000 a month, can you imagine it coming in for the rest of your life, regardless if you work or not?" While most of the guests responded positively to that idea, I doubt most thought it was possible. Besides, it seemed that most just wanted an extra $3,000 a month next month, rather than having to work for a few years for free, building a business, and then later on having the money come in forever. It is my guess that most people there were still thinking like employees of self-employed people who work for money, rather than business owners and investors who work for wealth from assets.

A Different Kind Of Money

One of the reasons the rich get richer is simply because the rich work for a different kind of money. The following diagram of a financial statement may help explain the difference:

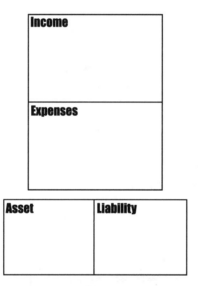

If you are not familiar with this diagram of a financial statement, or wish a further explanation of it, I suggest you either read *Rich Dad Poor Dad,* or talk to a friend who has read the book and ask them to explain it to you. It is a very important diagram to understand and is central to many of the lessons from my rich dad. As my rich dad often said, "My banker has never asked me for my report card. My banker asks me for my financial statement." Rich dad also said, "Your financial statement is your report card after you leave school. Your financial statement measures your financial IQ." That is how important this diagram is to anyone who wants to achieve financial freedom or great wealth.

A Difference In Focus

One of the ways to better explain the difference between an E and S and B and I is by using the financial statement. The difference between the left side of the quadrant and the right side of the quadrant is a difference in focus. The following explains what I mean:

Simply put, people in the E and S quadrant focus here:

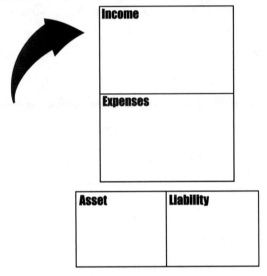

And people in the B and I quadrants focus here:

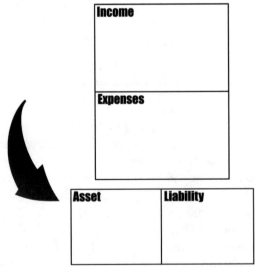

Are You Still Working For Money?

The primary difference shown by the financial statement is that the people in the E and S quadrants work for money. The people in the B and I quadrants focus on building or acquiring assets rather than working for money. That is why the wealth of a B or I person is higher than an E or S quadrant person is. If the B or I person stops working, the assets continue to make money for the B or I quadrant person.

The Three Types Of Assets

The three main types of assets found in an asset column are:

```
Income



Expenses



Asset              Liability
1. B quadrant
   businesses
2. Real estate
3. Paper assets
```

A Simple Plan To Financial Freedom

The simple plan my wife Kim and I used to retire young and retire rich was to, first, build a business and, second, to invest in real estate. As I said, it took us from 1985 to 1994, starting with nothing and retiring financially free without a single share of stock or mutual funds. That was our simple plan, and we followed our plan.

There have been people who have asked me, "Why did you build a business first?" There are three answers to that question. The *first answer* is that building a business allowed us to generate a lot of money. At the start of this book, I listed the 11 different ways a person can become rich, such as marrying someone for money. For Kim and I, the best way for us to become rich was to build a business. The *second answer* is because the tax laws of the United States are very favorable to people who earn their income in the B quadrant and punish people who earn their money in the E quadrant. Lastly, the *third answer* is building a business and investing in real estate: the plan that most of the truly rich follow.

How Can I Afford To Buy Real Estate?

After the stock market crash of 2000, many people began to wake up to the realization that stocks and mutual funds are risky. After the crash, many people began to wonder about investing in real estate. The problem was many people did not have enough money to invest in real estate or live in places where real estate is expensive. A question I am often asked today is, "How can I buy real estate when I barely earn enough money to pay the rent?"

My answer is always the same. I always say, "Keep your day time job and start building a part-time business. Once the business is making money, the second step is to keep your daytime job and begin to buy investment real estate with the extra-income from the business. That way you begin to build two assets classes rather than spending your life working for money.

Three Types Of Intelligence

Just as there are three different types of education required for financial success—academic, professional and financial—there are three different types of intelligence required for financial success in the real world. The three types of intelligence are:

1. Mental Intelligence: Generally, where IQ is measured in school.

2. Emotional Intelligence: It has been said that emotional intelligence is 25 times more powerful than mental intelligence. Examples of emotional intelligence are: keeping one's cool rather than arguing back; not getting married to someone you know in the long run will not be a good life partner; and delayed gratification, which is the opposite of instant gratification, the cause of many of today's financial problems.

3. Financial Intelligence: My rich dad said, "Your financial intelligence is measured on your personal financial statement. Your financial intelligence is measured by how much money you make, how much money you keep, how hard that money works for you, and how many generations you can pass on the money to."

Why Smart People Fail To Become Rich

One of the reasons many smart people, like my poor dad, fail to become rich, even though they have a high IQ and did well in school, is because they lack the *emotional intelligence* required for financial success and wealth accumulation. The four common signs of low emotional IQ are:

1. They get rich too slowly because they play the money game too cautiously. Because they are in a job in the E quadrant, they often pay a higher percentage of income in taxes; they fail to invest wisely, keeping their money in the bank, earning very little in interest; and the little they do earn in interest is taxed at the highest taxable rate.

2. Trying to get rich too quickly. This person lacks the emotional intelligence known as patience. This person often goes from job to job or hot new idea to hot new idea. They start something, get bored and quit.

3. Spends on impulse. This person's favorite form of exercise is going shopping. They shop until they drop. If they have money, they spend it on a whim. These people say, "Money seems to run through my fingers."

4. Cannot stand owning anything of value. In other words, this person only owns things or works at things that make them poor. For example, I have met several people who have invested in investment real estate. The moment they own it, they sell, take the earnings and pay off credit card bills or student loans or they buy a new boat or take a vacation. In other words, they hang on to things that have very little value and sell anything that has real value.

Many of these same people, rather than build a business, feel better working for someone else and working hard at something they will never own. The emotion of fear is so high that they would rather work for security rather than work for freedom.

Emotional Intelligence Is Essential To Financial Intelligence

This chapter started with my radio interview. The reason I started with this interview is that this young man was out of control emotionally. He was obviously very bright mentally, but his emotions were causing him to think irrationally. If you are out of control emotionally, your chances of solving your financial challenges are reduced.

Simply said, in the real world, emotional intelligence is more important than mental intelligence if you want to become rich. Having a *high emotional IQ* is essential to having a *high financial IQ*. Warren Buffet, America's richest investor says, "A person who cannot manage their emotions cannot manage their money."

> **"In the real world, emotional intelligence is more important than mental intelligence if you want to become rich."**

When I was younger, I was an emotional retard. Everything was "Live for today." That is one reason I did not achieve financial freedom until I was 47, even though I knew what to do. Whenever I acted up or got out of hand, wanting to either get rich quickly or quit because I was frustrated, rich dad would often say, "Come back when you've grown up. Then I'll get back to teaching you to be rich."

Do You Want To Improve Your Emotional IQ?

It has been my personal experience that the more my emotional IQ goes up, the better my life became. Being a former Marine, not only am I impulsive; I have also developed a very violent and quick temper. When I returned from Vietnam, my rich dad said, "Your hot temper and quick reaction may have kept you alive in Vietnam, but those same emotions will kill you in the world of business." Rich dad strongly suggested I work on improving my emotional IQ if I wanted to improve my financial IQ. As my control over my emotions improved, my marriage improved, my business skills improved and so did my investment skills. My health even improved, just by keeping my temper at bay, although at times it still takes control over me. The first step in increasing my emotional intelligence is to admit I need to improve it.

If you are like me, a person who can always use a little more emotional maturity, a network marketing business may be the best training ground for you. To me, one of the best values of a network marketing business is that it develops your emotional IQ. You raise your emotional IQ every time you deal with people who quit or people who lie, and everytime you overcome your own fears, your disappointments, your frustrations, and your own impatience to become a better person. In other words, a network marketing business is a great place to get to know yourself better and work on improving yourself.

Ask yourself this question: "How are my emotions interfering with my life? Are my emotions causing me to be...

1. Too shy?
2. Afraid of rejection?
3. Needing security?
4. Too impatient?
5. Too hot-tempered?
6. Addicted to something?

7. Too impulsive?
8. Too angry?
9. Too slow to change?
10. Lazy?
11. _____(your choice)?

Again, one of the great values of a network marketing business is that it will test your emotional intelligence and in many cases greatly improve it. Once you begin improving your emotional IQ, you will probably find other areas of your life improving. You will find it easier to talk to people, communicate more clearly, and handle their emotions more effectively. When you can do those things better, your business will grow faster. Being more patient, you have a better chance at being a better investor. By developing your emotional intelligence, your marriage may improve, if you are married or want to become married, and we all know how emotional a subject marriage can be. You may also become a better parent and hence raise better kids. Therefore, I would say that investing a number of years building a network marketing business might pay off in many other areas of your life. Why? Because life is a very emotional subject.

A Better Marriage

For Kim and me, our plan to become financially free was great for our marriage. Starting with nothing, we had a project we could both work on together. I would say handling the ups and downs of building a business offered many challenges to our marriage, yet in the end, it made our marriage stronger. We took risks together, took our losses together, and celebrated our wins together.

As stated earlier, our plan was simple. In 1985, Kim and I began building our business, starting with nothing. In 1991, we invested in our first piece of investment real estate only after the business was very profitable. In 1994, we sold our business, bought more real estate, and retired financially free for the rest of our lives. It was a simple plan and it made our lives simpler and happier. As most of us know, money is one of the main subjects for argument in a marriage. Today we have a better marriage, not so much because of the money, but because we built a business together. Instead of growing apart, we grew closer together as we became more emotionally mature. I hear many people say, "Oh, I could never work with my husband. I could not stand being around him that much." I can honestly say that I would not be as successful today without Kim and we would not have as great a marriage if we had worked at different jobs for different companies. If we had worked apart, we would have grown apart. Building businesses together and investing together made our marriage stronger because we had the time to work out our differences, we grew closer together, got to know each other better, began to respect each other more, matured emotionally together, and in the end, we became much happier with each other…and to me that is priceless. While we still have our differences, today we know our love for each other is greater than those differences. A happy marriage between two people is definitely due to emotional intelligence more than two people with good grades and good jobs earning a lot of money.

Why Some Successful Network Marketers Fail

Over the years I have met several successful network marketers who have built vast fortunes with their business. I have also met several network marketers who built a big business and then lost everything. Why? Again, the answer is found in emotional intelligence.

An example of a successful network marketer who failed is a person named Ray. Ray lives in Southern California. He worked for a health food store chain right after college and he was soon appointed to store manager. Ray, having a biochemistry degree, was very interested in health. One day a customer walked in and showed Ray this new product line of health products. Ray tried the products and they were great. Ray immediately went to his boss and asked him if the store could carry them. The boss said, "No." Being impatient and impulsive, Ray quit his job and jumped into this network marketing business opportunity.

For three years, Ray studied and learned the business. He struggled financially for a few years and then suddenly the lights went on: Ray had made it from the E quadrant to the mind-set of the B quadrant. His business exploded and soon he was making more money in a week than he was making in a year at his job at the health food store.

Soon Ray was on the stage talking to all the new people coming into the business. He was the new star. The trouble was that the stage and stardom went to his head. He became arrogant and cocky, a sign of low emotional intelligence. He began to argue with those who taught him the business, thinking he was smarter than they were because he had nicer cars, nicer homes, and more free-flowing cash. The money had truly gone to his head.

A new network marketing business was starting up. They too had an excellent health product line and they were looking for stars like Ray to defect and join their business. It did not take long for the new business owners to woo Ray away from the older more established company he had started with. Ray made the jump because he wanted to get in on the ground floor, get in early, and build a bigger business quicker. Ray also took many on his team with him.

Three years later Ray was broke. Why? There are two reasons I can find. One is that the owners of the new company were just like Ray. They were impatient and impulsive. They too wanted to get richer quicker. The second reason is that just like Ray, the new company owners were poor money managers that lived high on the hog, looking good, flashing cash, and talking trash. Rather than reinvest in their business, and reinvest in real estate, they bought the symbols of wealth rather than acquired real wealth. Do you remember earlier in this chapter when I mentioned that poor people often feel uncomfortable with things of real value? Ray and the founders of the new business were in that category, I believe. That is why Ray and the owner of the new company failed to buy real wealth. Instead, they bought fast cars, fast women, and went out of business and into bankruptcy court at high speed. Birds of a feather do flock together.

Today Ray is still hopping from one new network marketing business to another. Every time I see him, he has a new business opportunity and a new product line to promote. Ray learned to build a network marketing business, but he failed to become successful in the business. He failed because his emotions did his thinking.

Don't Be A Frog

Now, I am not saying that it is wrong to change network marketing companies. I know it happens. I am saying that many people are like Ray, who go from company to company looking for the perfect business, the perfect product line, and easy money. Many people do that because they fail to develop their emotional intelligence, which is, in my opinion, one of the main reasons to go into the business. In other words, it is OK to leave a business, but do it for the right reasons rather than emotional reasons. Hopping from lily pad to lily pad may be good for frogs, but it is not good for business owners. As a friend of mine said, "The trouble with being a frog is that not only do you spend your day chasing bugs; you also have to eat the bugs you catch." The message is, once you find a network marketing business that is right for you, give the business and yourself time to grow up together. Don't be a frog chasing bugs.

Why Successful Network Marketers Become More Successful

It was also a pleasure to meet some very successful network marketing business owners, many of whom are far more successful than me and even my rich dad. For me, the pleasure was to find that the formula for success in the network marketing business is the same formula my rich dad taught me. The formula is as follows:

1. Build a business. Getting a business off the ground usually takes about five years. I know it can take less time and it can take longer. However, a business is like a child: it takes time to grow.

2. Reinvest in the business. The reason this is important is that this step is the one that Ray and many others do not like to do. Rather than reinvest, they spend their money as fast as they get it. They are soon buying on credit— nice cars, nice homes, nice clothes and nice vacations. Instead of helping their child grow, they steal the kid's lunch money and the kid begins to starve.

Unfortunately, stories about people like Ray are common in every business. One of the main reasons why so few people in America are rich, even if they make a lot of money, is simply because they spend their kid's lunch money on toys and things that make their ego feel good.

How Businesses Reinvest

As a traditional business, richdad.com has been reinvesting by spending millions of dollars on improving our Web site, building our own live Web games *CASHFLOW 101* and *CASHFLOW for Kids,* the game and school curriculum that is given to schools for free. These are examples of a traditional business reinvesting into the business. Another example may be building a warehouse, adding trucks to the fleet, or spending money on national advertising.

In a network marketing business, reinvesting may mean expanding your business from 10 people to 20 people. It can also mean investing some time in helping your downline get deeper. The beauty of most network marketing businesses is that it does not require that much money to reinvest into your business.

One last point is that a true business owner never stops investing and reinvesting to build the business. The reason so many people fail to achieve great wealth in any business is simply that they fail to reinvest continually in the business.

3. Invest in real estate. Why real estate? Two reasons. One is because the tax laws (loopholes) are written in favor of business owners who invest in real estate. The second reason is your banker loves to lend you money for real estate. Try asking your banker for a 30-year loan at 6.5 percent to buy mutual funds or stocks. They'll laugh you out of their bank.

A word of caution: The reason I suggest building a business first is investing in real estate takes time, education, experience and money. If you do not have the extra steady income and the tax advantages that come with a B quadrant business, real estate is either too risky or too slow. The reason it is too risky is that mistakes in real estate, especially in property management, can be very expensive. The reason many people fail to become rich in real estate or get rich too slowly is simply that they do not have the excess cash business owners often have. In reality, the best real estate deals are usually expensive. If you don't have money, the only real estate deals are often deals people with money have passed on. Today I meet many people looking for "nothing down" real estate investments. While they do exist, the main reason they look for them is that they have "nothing to put down." If you lack real estate education, experience, and money, putting nothing down could be the most expensive investment of your life. So build a business first, reinvest in the business second, and third, buy real estate.

> **"So build a business first, reinvest in the business second, and third, buy real estate."**

4. Buy luxuries. For most of our marriage, Kim and I did not live in a big house or drive nice cars. For years, we lived in a small house that cost us about $400 a month in mortgage payments. While we lived in that small house and drove average cars, we were building our business and investing in real estate. Today we live in a much larger home and we have six cars between us, but we also have far more money coming in from our assets such as businesses and real estate. My rich dad's simple rule of thumb was, build a business, reinvest in your business so it grows, invest in real estate, and then have your business and real estate buy your luxuries. In other words, work to build or buy your assets, and then have your assets buy your luxuries.

Today, even though Kim and I have our big house and our six cars, we can still afford to stop working for the rest of our lives because we do not have jobs; we have assets. Today we work because we love what we do. On top of that, we get richer and richer simply because we follow my rich dad's simple four-step formula for real wealth and ever-increasing wealth. We build businesses, reinvest in business, invest in real estate, and then our assets buy luxuries.

Why Don't Most People Become Rich?

Why don't most people follow this plan, even though it is a simple plan? The answer in most cases is again found in emotional intelligence. Most people lack the patience, the discipline, and the willingness to delay gratification to follow such a plan. Most people earn money and then spend money. Therefore, it is not a matter of mental IQ or financial IQ. It is a matter of emotional IQ. In fact, the easiest of all three IQ's is financial IQ, which explains why so many people who did not do well in school are rich. Therefore, in my opinion, the bridge to financial IQ is emotional IQ, and a network marketing business can help anyone in developing that intelligence.

When Do You Buy Paper Assets?

Many people ask me, "When do you buy paper assets such as stocks, bonds and mutual funds?" My answer is my rich dad's answer. Years ago, rich dad said to me, "The best asset is a business. The reason I put a business as number one is simply that it is the best asset to own, if you are smart enough to own one. The second is real estate, and third are paper assets. The reason paper assets are last is simply because they are the easiest to buy but the riskiest to own. If you don't believe me about the risk in paper assets, just go ask your banker to give you a 30-year mortgage to buy them."

Therefore, my answer to people today is my rich dad's answer. The reason paper assets are last is because they are the easiest to buy but the riskiest to own. One more reason is that I can buy insurance for catastrophic loss on a business or real estate. Very few people know how to buy insurance for stocks and I do not know of any insurance for mutual funds...but there might be.

Why People Are Not Happy At Work

A friend who is a trained and experienced mental health worker said to me, "One of the causes of happiness is the word control. The more control you have, the happier you become. On the flip side, if you are out of control or lose control, you often become unhappy." The example he gave was a person rushing to the airport and suddenly he finds himself stuck in a mile-long traffic jam. Creeping along in traffic with no way to get off the freeway, he realizes he is going to miss his plane and his cheerful mood disappears. The reason the person becomes unhappy is that he has no control over the traffic jam. The summary of his lesson was, "Control and happiness are closely related."

Going back to the caller on the radio at the start of this chapter, I would say he was not happy. One of the reasons I believe he was unhappy is because he had lost control over his life. Although he had what he believes is a secure job, he has no control over his finances. He has also lost control over his investments in stocks and mutual funds. In the world today, especially after the stock market crash, the economy weakening, and the September 11 terrorist attack, many people feel they have lost control and that leads to unhappiness. One of the great values in building a network marketing business and then investing in real estate is that they can give you back control over your life. If you have more control, you have more happiness, and happiness is a very valuable emotion to have in your life.

In Summary

So the question is, "Are you working for money or working for wealth?" If it is time to start working for wealth, I have two suggestions. Looking at the CASHFLOW Quadrant below, I suggest the following:

Start a network marketing business part-time

Play rich dad's *CASHFLOW 101* game and learn how to invest

In your spare time, if you will do both for the next three to five years, I believe your financial future will be far brighter than if you did what most people do, which is to cling to job security and invest their money in mutual funds. How can anyone be happy when he or she has given control of his or her financial life away to someone else? In addition, in a few years, if you are successful in both the B and the I quadrants, you will be working for wealth instead of working for money.

The Next Value

The next chapter will go into the value of having your dreams come true. For those who have played *CASHFLOW 101,* you may recall that the first step before playing the game is to choose your dream. Rich dad always said, "Start with your dreams and work backwards." I have left the best for last because now that you know you can acquire great wealth in your lifetime, you may want to dream bigger dreams.

CHAPTER 10

Value # 8: Living Your Dreams

"Many people don't have dreams," my rich dad said.
"Why?" I asked.
"Because dreams cost money," he said.

Rekindling The Dream

My wife Kim and I went to a gathering where a top producer in a network marketing company was showing off his 17,000 square foot mansion, with an eight-car garage, as well as the eight cars to fill it, his limousine, and all his other toys. The house and toys were impressive, but the thing that really impressed me was that the city had named the street his house was on after him. When I asked him how he got the city to do that, he said, "Easy, I donated money to build a new elementary school and a library. When I did that, the city allowed me to name the street after my family." At that point, I realized that his dream was far bigger than my dream. I have never dreamed of having a street named after me or donating enough money to build a school and a library. Leaving his home that night, I realized that it was time for me to increase the size of my dreams.

One of the more important values I have found in good network marketing companies is that they stress the importance of going for and living your dreams. The top producer we were visiting was not showing off his material goods merely to show off. He and his wife were speaking to the group about the lifestyle they had achieved in order to inspire the group to live their dreams. It was not about the big house, the toys or how much they cost. It was about inspiring others to go for their dreams.

Killing The Dream

In *Rich Dad Poor Dad*, I wrote about my poor dad constantly saying, "I can't afford it." I also wrote that my rich dad forbade his son and me from saying those words. Instead, he required us to say, "How can I afford it?" As simple as those statements are, the difference between them was very important to my rich dad. He said, "Asking yourself 'How can I afford things?' allows you to have bigger and bigger dreams."

Rich dad also said, "Be aware of people who want to kill your dreams. There is nothing worse than a friend or loved one killing your dreams." There are people who may innocently or not so innocently, say things such as:

1. "You can't do that."
2. "That is too risky. Do you know how many people fail?"
3. "Don't be silly. Where do you come up with such ideas?"
4. "If it is such a good idea, why hasn't someone else done it before?"
5. "Oh, I tried that years ago. Let me tell you why it won't work."

I have noticed that people who kill other people's dreams are people who have given up on their own dreams.

Why Dreams Are Important

My rich dad explained the importance of dreams in this way: "Being rich and being able to afford a big house are not important. What is important is striving, learning, and doing your best to develop your personal power to afford the big house. It is who you become in the process of affording the big house that is important. People who dream small dreams continue to live lives as small people."

> **"People who dream small dreams continue to live lives as small people."**

As my rich dad said, the home was not what was important. My wife Kim and I have owned two very large homes, and I agree that it was not the size of the house or becoming rich that was important. The size of the dream was what was important. When my wife and I were broke, we set a goal that when we had made over $1 million, we would buy a big house. When our business grossed over $1 million, we bought our first big house and then sold it soon after. We sold it because we had moved on to achieving a new dream. In other words, the house and earning $1 million were not the dream. The house and money were the symbols of becoming people who could achieve our dreams. Today, we again own a big home and, again, the home is just the symbol of the dream we achieved. Our big house is not the dream; it is who we became in the process that is the dream.

Rich dad said it this way: "Big people have big dreams and small people have small dreams. If you want to change who you are, begin by changing the size of your dream." When I was broke and lost most of my money, my rich dad said, "Never let this temporary financial setback diminish the size of your dream. It is the vision of your dream that will pull you through this rough period of life." He also said, "Broke is temporary and poor is eternal. Even if you are broke, it does not cost you anything to dream of being rich. Many poor people are poor because they have given up on dreaming."

Different Types Of Dreamers

When I was in high school, my rich dad explained that there were five kinds of dreamers:

1. Dreamers who dream in the past. Rich dad said there are many people whose greatest achievements in life are behind them. Al Bundy of TV's sitcom *Married With Children* is a classic example of someone whose dreams are behind him. For those who may not be familiar with the show, Al Bundy is a grown man who still re-lives his days in high school when he was a football star who scored four touchdowns in one game. That is an example of someone who continues to dream in the past.

Rich dad would say, "A person who dreams in the past is a person whose life is over. That person needs to create a dream in the future in order to come back to life."

It is not just ex-football stars who live in the past; it is also people who still revel in getting good grades, being prom king or queen, graduating from a prestigious university, or being in the military. In other words, their best days are behind them.

2. Dreamers who dream only small dreams. Rich dad said, "These types of dreamers will dream only small dreams because they want to feel confident they can achieve them. The problem is, even though they know they can achieve them, they never do achieve them."

This type of dreamer did not make much sense to me until one day I asked this man, "If you had all the money in the world, where would you travel?"

His reply was, "I would fly to California to visit my sister. I haven't seen her in 14 years, and I would love to see her, especially before her children get any older. That would be my dream vacation."

I then said, "But that would only cost you about $500. Why don't you do that today?"

"Oh I will, but not today. I'm just too busy right now."

After meeting this individual, I realized that this type of dreamer is more common than I thought. These people live their lives having dreams they know they can achieve, but they never seem to get around to living their dreams. Later in life, you can hear them say, "You know, I should have done that years ago, but I just never got around to doing it."

My rich dad said, "These types of dreamers are often the most dangerous. They live like turtles, tucked away in their own quiet padded room. If you knock on the shell and peek in one of the openings, they often lunge out and bite you." The lesson is let dreaming turtles dream. Most aren't going anywhere and that is perfectly fine with them.

3. Dreamers who have achieved their dreams and have not set a new dream. A friend of mine once said to me, "Twenty years ago, I dreamed of becoming a doctor. I became a doctor and now I am just bored with life. I enjoy being a doctor but something is missing."

This is an example of someone who has successfully achieved his dream and continues to live in the dream. Boredom usually is a sign that it is time for a new dream. My rich dad would say, "Many people are in professions they dreamed of in high school. The problem is they have been out of high school for years. It is time for a new dream and a new adventure."

4. Dreamers who dream big dreams but do not have a plan on how to achieve them...so they wind up achieving nothing. I think we all know someone in this category. These people say, "I've just had a major break-through. Let me tell you about my new plan," or, "This time things will be different," or, "I'm turning over a new leaf," or, "I'm going to work harder, pay off my bills, and invest," or, "I just heard of a new company coming to town, and they are looking for someone with my qualifications. This could be my big break."

My rich dad said, "Very few people achieve their dreams on their own. People like this often try to achieve a lot, but they try to do it on their own. People like this should keep dreaming big, find a plan, and find a team that will help them make their dreams come true."

5. Dreamers who dream big achieve those dreams and go on to dream bigger dreams. I think that most of us would like to be this kind of person. I know I would.

One of the most refreshing things that happened to me while looking into some of the network marketing businesses was that I found myself dreaming even bigger dreams. The business encourages people to dream big dreams and achieve their big dreams. Many traditional businesses don't want people to dream personal dreams.

Too many times, I meet people who have friends or work for businesses that actively kill a person's dreams. I support the network marketing industry because it is an industry made up of people who truly want people to dream big dreams and then it supports those people in creating a business plan, providing the training, the discipline, and the support to have their dreams come true.

In Summary

If you are a person with big dreams and would love to support others in achieving their big dreams, then the network marketing business is definitely a business for you. You can start your business part-time at first, and then as your business grows, you can help other people start their part-time business. This is a value worth having—a business and people who help others make their dreams come true.

What Are Your Big Dreams?

At this time, it is important that you take a moment to think, dream, and then write down your dreams. The following space is the place for you to look deep into yourself and put your dreams down on paper.

_____

_____

_____

_____

_____

_____

_____

_____

After you have written your dreams down, you may want to discuss your dreams with someone who will support you having everything you want. That may be the person who gave you this book.

A Little Added Value

This concludes my personal chapters on what I feel are the eight hidden values found in a network marketing business. In the Appendices are three additional "hidden values." Two very important women in my life offer these additional "hidden values" they feel are important in building a business.

The first person is my wife Kim. Kim writes about the value of marriage and business.

The second person is my business partner and co-author of the Rich Dad books, Sharon L. Lechter. Sharon writes about the impact of building a family business and how you can use the same tax advantages the rich use. Her son Phillip works in the business of richdad.com and he has been a tremendous asset to the business. Not only is he an asset, Sharon, who is a brilliant businesswoman, has the advantage of having more time to help educate and guide her son in the world of business.

Value #9: Marriage And Business

By Kim Kiyosaki

Robert and I had our first date in February 1984 in Honolulu, Hawaii. That evening he asked me, "What do you want to do in life?" I said, "I want to have my own business." At the time, I was managing a magazine in Honolulu. Robert said, "If you want, I'll teach you what I know and what my rich dad taught me." Within the month we had started a new (my first) business together.

We designed a unique logo, embroidered it on shirts and jackets, and traveled throughout the U.S. selling our products. The real purpose of this business was to fund our education for one year (attending business seminars, meetings and conferences across the country) while we prepared for the next business we were about to build. We completed our one-year goal and closed our shirt and jacket business.

In December 1984, we sold everything we had in Hawaii and moved to Southern California, and set out to build our next business. Within two months, we had gone through all the savings we had. We were broke. We knocked on friend's doors and asked to stay the night. We slept on the beach. Some nights we slept in an old borrowed beat-up Toyota. My family thought we were crazy. Our friends thought we were crazy. Moreover, sometimes we even thought we were crazy.

To be candid, I don't know if we would have made it if we didn't have each other. There were nights when we would just hold each other—providing a little shelter from the storm. Was I scared? Yes. Was I uncertain? Yes. Did I think at times that we wouldn't make it? Absolutely! Nevertheless, we were determined to keep going. Moreover, we did.

The thing that kept us going was our determination to build our business, and more importantly, not to go back to a paycheck. Getting a job at that point would have been the easy thing to do. However, to us that would be going backwards. We knew what we wanted; we just weren't sure how to get there...yet (This seems to be a common theme throughout our lives).

The bottom line is we didn't go back. We stayed true to our dream. We built our business—an international education business operating in seven countries. We sold that business in 1994, and today, our time is primarily spent between investing and our Rich Dad business.

What I Really Wanted

There was one thing, however, I didn't tell Robert the night of our first date. What else I wanted along with my own business was a partner/spouse who was also my business partner. Building a business is all-consuming. I wanted to grow together with my partner, not grow apart because we never saw each other, because we had different focuses, or because we were moving in different directions. I did not want to be like so many other married couples I had seen at restaurants who just sit there in silence because they having nothing to discuss. Robert and I have conversations that are exhilarating, frustrating, loving, confronting...but we always have plenty to talk about and what's most rewarding for me is that the personal growth I experience from growing my business each day I get to share and experience with Robert.

Personal Growth

When I look back on that first year of our business, I would say it was the worst year of our lives. The stress was extreme, my self-esteem took a beating, and our relationship was not always peaceful. However, in retrospect it was probably the best thing that could have happened to us. By getting through those hard times, it helped to make us who we are today. As a result, Robert and I individually are much stronger, more confident and definitely smarter from all our learnings. In addition, the love, the respect and the joy of our marriage are beyond my wildest dreams.

Working Together

In the network marketing industry, I see many couples building their businesses together. To me this is a perfect business for couples that want to go into business together for several reasons:

1. It's a business you can both begin part-time
2. You dictate the hours to fit your schedules
3. The industry supports families in business together
4. Many of the most successful people in the industry are couples
5. The education many network marketing companies offer allows couples to learn and grow together

These are some strong pluses for couples. Now I'll be honest: being in business with your spouse is not necessarily the easiest thing in the world by any means. Yes, Robert and I have had our moments, but I will say it has been the most rewarding for us. We have built several businesses together. Years ago we thought it might be better that we each have our own primary business in different arenas. However, when we weighed our options, it was crystal clear that we wanted to build our businesses together, not apart.

For me, what is important is that Robert and I share common values, goals and ultimately a common mission. Because we are always learning together, we are growing together. We even have a policy that if one of us attends an educational seminar or conference then we both attend it. What's fun for us is that we always talk about our businesses—figuring out ways to make them better, meeting new people and exploring new ideas.

Working with your spouse may not be for everyone. I recognize that. However, for me, I wouldn't have it any other way.

Best wishes,

Kim Kiyosaki

Value #10: The Family Business

By Sharon L. Lechter, C.P.A.

In *The Business School For People Who Like Helping People,* Robert and I outline several of the primary benefits of starting a network marketing business.

1. There is a low entry cost to get started in a network marketing business.
2. No formal education or degree is required to qualify for most of the companies.
3. The industry is open to everyone, regardless of your gender, age or race.
4. Companies provide established systems, already proven successful, available for you to use to build your business.
5. Many companies provide good education and training programs to help you become successful.
6. There are mentors, successful in the business, ready to assist you in your journey.
7. You can start a network marketing business part-time and build it while you keep your job.
8. There are many tax advantages available to a business owner, which are not available to you as an employee.

There is another important benefit, or value, of a network marketing business. That is the value a successful network marketing business brings to the family. Robert asked me to share my personal thoughts about the value to the family in light of my personal experience.

My Family

Family is the most important thing to me. My husband, Michael and our children, Phillip, Shelly and Rick are the center of my life. However, early in our marriage as Michael and I grew more successful professionally, we found we were spending less and less time with our children due to the demands of our businesses. We were both workaholics and we knew that something had to change.

While Michael continued working longer and longer hours, I found ways to work from home to make sure that I was around more for our children. I was very fortunate that I could choose to combine my professional pursuits with the concerns I had as a mother. For instance, when my children were small I was concerned about their lack of interest in reading so I went to work with a friend who invented talking books for children.

When our oldest son, Phillip went off to college and got into credit card debt before December of his freshman year, I was devastated. As a C.P.A., I felt I had taught my children about money, but my son's experience showed that I had not done a good enough job. I turned my focus to getting financial education into the school system.

Even though I was around more, my children still missed spending time with their dad…and he missed much of their youth. We seldom took time for family vacations. We were very successful and had become rich by conventional standards but at the expense of time with the family. Many, if not most, of our friends found themselves in the same situation: the more professional success they enjoyed, the less family time they had together. We all thought this type of family life was normal.

Three years later, Michael introduced me to Robert, and everything changed.

Rich Dad And The Lechters

In working with Robert in developing the Rich Dad books, games and other materials Michael and I have had the opportunity to involve our children along the way and have seen their lives changed dramatically through the process. Not only have they learned the Rich Dad lessons to help them in their own lives, but also our relationship with our children has strengthened because of working and learning together. We are honored and very proud to have Phillip as an important part of the Rich Dad team. It is so rewarding to work with Phil and see him grow within our company. By following the Rich Dad lessons of working to learn, not to earn, Phillip has developed the experience and knowledge to help lead the company to its next level. However, the more personal reward is that our family bond truly grows stronger as we learn and work together toward a common goal.

The experience of sharing the Rich Dad message with our children and seeing them internalize it has been incredible. It has become our family business.

Create Your Own Family Business

How does this relate to network marketing? Over the last few years, I have had the opportunity to get to know many wonderful and successful people and families in the network marketing industry and I found many qualities they all shared:

1. All are very family-focused.
2. All value the extra time their success allows them to spend with their family.
3. The children learn the benefits of the network marketing business from experiencing it with their parents.
4. They take many more family vacations and family business trips than we ever did.
5. The children learn the benefit of passive income and financial education at early ages.
6. The children often choose to participate in the business on their own.
7. Many set family goals and work together for a common goal.
8. Often, one parent will continue working their full-time job while the other parent begins building the network marketing business on the side.
9. The very nature of the industry promotes family togetherness and unity.

True Wealth Is Measured In Time, Not Money

I didn't have enough time with my kids while they were growing up, and now that they are grown, I can truly appreciate the value of the family-centered focus of successful people within the network marketing industry. What a gift to be able to build your business WITH your family instead of FOR your family.

Rich Dad defines wealth in time, not money. The more successful you become, the more time you will have and the more freedom you will have to spend with your family.

Congratulations on selecting a family-focused business. May your family share the gifts of love and togetherness from your success!

All the best,

Sharon Lechter

Value #11: How You Can Use The Same Tax Advantages The Rich Use

By Sharon L. Lechter, C.P.A.

Mind Your Own Business

Are you minding your own business? If you are an employee, it is not what you do from 8 to 5 that counts. It is what you do with your paycheck after you receive it that counts.

In other words, what you do from 8 to 5 is your profession or your job. What you do with your paycheck is your business. Too many people rely on their employer or their government to take care of them.

Who Are You Working For?

Let's say you have a salary of $48,000 per year. In other words you are paid $4,000 per month to mind your employer's business. Then you get your paycheck and it is for only $2,500. The $1,500 of withholding taxes is you minding Uncle Sam's business. Then you have to make your mortgage payment to the bank of $1,500, which represents you minding the bank's business. Oh, and let's not forget that credit card balance that you let get away from you. That $400 payment is you working for the credit card company. Another $440 goes for living expenses. What are you left with? At the end of the month you are lucky to have $160 for investment, that's $1 per hour that you are earning working for yourself.

Let's review:

Salary	$4,000	You working for your boss
less:		
Taxes	$1,500	You working for the government
Mortgage	$1,500	You working for the bank
Credit Card	$ 400	You working for the credit card company
Living	$ 440	You working for your creditors
Net	$ 160	You working for you!

It isn't how much money you make that counts, it is how much money you keep. Most people work for everyone else but themselves. Financial struggle is often a direct result of people working all their lives for someone else, and at the end of their working days they have nothing left for themselves.

To become financially secure, you need to mind your own business. Your business revolves around your asset column as opposed to your income column. Learn the difference between assets and liabilities by reading *Rich Dad Poor Dad* and start buying or building assets. The rich focus on their asset column while everyone else focuses on their income column.

Start minding your own business. Keep your daytime job, but start buying real assets, not liabilities or personal effects that have no real value once you get them home. Build your asset column and keep it strong. Once a dollar goes into it, never let it come out. Think of each dollar as your employee. Money in your asset column is money working for you instead of you working for money.

Many people think we are telling people to quit their jobs. For some people that may be the right answer, but it is not the right answer for everybody. We want people to take more responsibility for their own financial decisions. Realize that you have the choice with every dollar you receive how you are going to spend it.

It is very difficult to get rich on an extra $160 per month. So what choices do you have?

1. Work overtime?
2. Get a second job?
3. Downsize your house?
4. Start your own business on the side, part-time?

All of these options will give you more money, but which one might help you on your way to wealth the quickest? The first two, working overtime and getting a second job just make your situation worse and result in you spending more time working for others. The third will help reduce your mortgage payment each month and may be a viable option for you, but it is still a one-time reduction in expenses. Let's examine the fourth option, starting your own business on the side, even if you need to keep your job temporarily.

The difference between the employee and the business owner is that the employee pays taxes FIRST and then pays expenses. The business owner pays expenses FIRST and then pays taxes. The business owner will always pay less tax than the employee simply because they can reduce the income amount they have to pay tax on!

As a business owner you can also take advantage of tax deductions that are not available to employees. With proper advice and documentation, you might even be able to convert some personal expenses into legitimate deductible business expenses. Of course, your business must have a legitimate money making business purpose other than just saving taxes. Here are just some of the business deductions that you might be able to take advantage of:

1. Home office expenses
2. Business equipment (computers, cell phones)
3. Office supplies
4. Internet and telephone service
5. Software and subscriptions
6. Mileage and other auto expenses
7. Travel, meals and entertainment
8. Business gifts
9. Medical insurance premiums
10. Medical expenses
11. Tuition and seminar educational expenses
12. Child labor expenses
13. Furniture

Look for expenses like these that may be tax deductible if they meet the criteria set by the IRS as outlined in the Internal Revenue Code Section 162(a): "There shall be allowed as a deduction, all the ordinary and necessary expenses paid or incurred during the taxable year in carrying on any trade or business."

As a business owner you have additional advantage of having the use of the money from your business to reinvest into building your business before you pay taxes, instead of the government taking its share even before you receive your income. We do not expect you to become a tax expert, but by becoming more aware of the tax laws and deductions available to business owners you can maximize your income and minimize your taxes legally. It is very important to seek competent tax advisors to help you create the strategy that suits your business and investment needs and to know what questions to ask of your advisors,

Have Fun Minding Your Own Business!

Sharon Lechter

Selected Quotes

"If you want to be rich, you need to be a business owner and an investor."

"Since you did not become rich from building a network marketing business, why do you recommend that others get into the business? It is because I did not gain my fortune from building a network marketing business that I can be a bit more objective about the industry. This book describes what I see as the real value of a network marketing business...a value that goes beyond just the potential of making a lot of money. I finally found a business with a heart and a deep caring for people."

"If I had to do it all over again, rather than build an old-style type of business, I would have started building a network marketing business."

"A network marketing business is a new and revolutionary way to achieve wealth."

"The richest people in the world build networks. Everyone else is trained to look for work."

"Network marketing gives millions of people throughout the world the opportunity to take control of their lives and their financial future."

"A network marketing business is a business with people who are there to help you become richer."

"Network marketing systems are fairer than previous systems for acquiring wealth."

"A network marketing system, a system I often call a *personal franchise* or an *invisible big business network,* is a very democratic way of wealth creation. The system is open to anyone who has drive, determination and perseverance."

"Many companies in the network marketing industry are offering millions of people the same business education my rich dad taught me: the opportunity of building your own network rather than spending your life working for a network."

"The network marketing industry continues to grow faster than franchises or traditional big businesses."

"A network marketing business is for people who want to enter the world of the B quadrant, either part-time or full-time."

"Simply put, a network marketing business, with its low cost of entry and great training programs, is an idea whose time has come."

"There is far more to a network marketing business than just the chance to make some extra money."

"A network marketing business is the perfect business for people who like helping other people."

"I recommend a network marketing business for its life-changing system of education."

"Many companies in the network marketing industry are really business schools for the people, rather than business schools that take smart kids and train them to be employees of the rich."

"Many network marketing companies are really business schools that teach values not found in traditional business schools...values such as the best way to become rich is to teach yourself and other people to become business owners, rather than teach them to be a loyal employee working for the rich."

"Network marketing businesses are business schools for people who want to learn the real world skills of an entrepreneur, rather than the skills of an employee who wants to become a highly paid mid-level manager in the corporate world."

"A network marketing business is based upon the leaders pulling people up, while a traditional corporate or government business is based upon only promoting a few and keeping the masses of employees content with a steady paycheck."

"I found in network marketing companies an education system designed to *draw* out the rich person in you."

"In the world of network marketing, you are encouraged to learn by making mistakes, correcting, and getting smarter mentally as well as emotionally."

"If you love to lead by teaching, influencing others to find their own world of financial abundance without having to beat the competition, then a network marketing business may be right for you."

"If you are a person who is terrified of making mistakes and afraid of failing, then I believe a network marketing business with a great educational program is especially good for you."

"One of the beauties of network marketing is that it gives you the opportunity to face your fears, deal with them, overcome them, and let the winner in you win."

"The network marketing business encourages people to dream big dreams and achieve their big dreams."

"A network marketing business provides a large support group of like-minded people with the same core values—the values of the B quadrant—to assist you while you make your transition to the B quadrant."

"After you have built your business, and you have strong cash flow, then you can begin investing in other assets."

ROBERT T. KIYOSAKI

Robert Kiyosaki is an investor, entrepreneur, educator and author.

Born and raised in Hawaii, Robert Kiyosaki is a fourth-generation Japanese-American. After graduating from college in New York, Robert joined the Marine Corps and served in Vietnam as an officer and helicopter gunship pilot. Following the war, Robert worked for the Xerox Corporation in sales. In 1977, he started a company that brought the first nylon and Velcro 'surfer wallets' to market. And in 1985 he founded an international education company that taught business and investing to tens of thousands of students throughout the world.

In 1994 Robert sold his business and through his investments, was able to retire at the age of 47.

During his short-lived retirement, Robert wrote the bestselling book *Rich Dad Poor Dad,* which to date has sold over 17 million copies worldwide. The success of *Rich Dad Poor Dad* paved the way for the Rich Dad series of books —currently ten books in total. Most all of these books have earned spots on the bestseller lists of the *New York Times, The Wall Street Journal, Business Week, USA Today* and others.

Prior to becoming a bestselling author, Robert created the educational board game CASHFLOW® 101 to teach individuals the financial and investment strategies that his rich dad spent years teaching him. It was those same strategies that allowed Robert to retire at age 47. Hundreds of "Cashflow Clubs," independent of The Rich Dad® Company, have sprung up throughout the world. Thousands of people get together on a regular basis and play CASHFLOW 101.

With the launch of the electronic version of CASHFLOW 101, members of the Rich Dad community around the world can unite in playing and learning together—on-line. CASHFLOW 202, the advanced game, is now gaining great popularity in both the board game and electronic versions.

In Robert's words, "We go to school to learn to work hard for money. I write books and create products that teach people how to have money work hard for them. Then they can enjoy the luxuries of this great world we live in."

The Rich Dad Company is the collaborative effort of Robert Kiyosaki, Kim Kiyosaki and Sharon Lechter, who, in 1997, set out to elevate the financial literacy of people throughout the world.

KIM KIYOSAKI

Kim Kiyosaki entered the business world in a position with a top Honolulu advertising agency and by age 25 she was operating a Honolulu magazine that served the city's business community. It didn't take long for Kim's entrepreneurial spirit to surface and two years later she ventured into her first business: a clothing company with national distribution.

Not long after launching that company, Kim joined Robert Kiyosaki as a partner in a company that taught entrepreneurial business throughout the world. That business grew to support 11 offices in seven countries, presenting business seminars to tens of thousands of attendees.

In 1989, Kim began her real estate investing career with the purchase of a small two-bedroom, one-bath rental house in Portland, Oregon. Today, Kim's real estate investment company buys, sells and manages millions of dollars worth of property. Kim strongly advocates and encourages women to get into the world of investing. According to Kim, "Investing can ultimately lead women to freedom—freedom of never having to be dependent on anyone for their financial well-being."

Kim and Robert, who married in 1984, sold their education seminar business in 1994 and 'retired.' In 1997, Kim and Robert—with partner and *Rich Dad Poor Dad* co-author Sharon Lechter—founded the company that would take the Rich Dad® message and mission of financial literacy—through books, games and other educational tools—to international recognition and acclaim.

SHARON L. LECHTER, C.P.A.

Sharon Lechter C.P.A., co-author of the Rich Dad book series and co-founder of Rich Dad's Organization, has dedicated her professional efforts to the field of education. She graduated with honors from Florida State University with a degree in accounting and started her career with Coopers & Lybrand. Sharon has held various management positions with computer, insurance and publishing companies while maintaining her professional credentials as a CPA.

Sharon and husband Michael Lechter have been married for over 20 years and are parents to three children, Phillip, Shelly and William. As her children grew, she became actively involved in their education and served in leadership positions in their schools. She became a vocal activist in the areas of mathematics, computers, reading and writing education.

In 1989 she joined forces with the inventor of the first electronic 'talking book' and helped him expand the electronic book industry to a multi-million dollar international market.

Today she remains a pioneer in developing new technologies to bring education into children's lives in ways that are innovative, challenging and fun. As co-author of the Rich Dad books she focuses her efforts in the arena of financial education.

"Our current educational system has not been able to keep pace with the global and technological changes in the world today," Sharon states. "We must teach our young people the skills – both scholastic and financial – that they need to not only survive but to flourish in the world."

A committed philanthropist, Sharon 'gives back' to the world communities as both a volunteer and a benefactor. She directs the Foundation for Financial Literacy and is a strong advocate of education and the need for improved financial literacy. Sharon and Michael were honored by Childhelp USA, national organization founded to eradicate child abuse in the United States, as recipients of the 2002 "Spirit of the Children" Award. And, in May of 2002, Sharon was named Chairman of the Board for the Phoenix chapter of Childhelp USA.

As an active member of Women's Presidents Organization, she enjoys networking with other professional women across the country.

Robert Kiyosaki, her business partner and friend, says "Sharon is one of the few natural entrepreneurs I have ever met. My respect for her continues to grow every day that we work together."

Time Warner Book Group Chairman, Larry Kirshbaum, has stated: "What Sharon and Robert have accomplished with Rich Dad is a feat that is unprecedented in the publishing arena."

BLAIR SINGER

The message is clear. In order to be rich and to succeed in business you have to be able to sell and teach others how to sell. Secondly, to build a successful business you have to know how to build a championship team that can win no matter what. Blair Singer has helped increase the revenues of companies and individuals all over the world through giving them the secrets to implementing those critical components.

If the owner or leader of an organization can sell and instill that spirit of ownership, accountability and team into the culture of the business, incomes soar. If they cannot, it fails. Blair's work with thousands of individuals and organizations has allowed them to experience unparalleled growth, return on investment and financial freedom.

He is a facilitator of personal and organizational change, a trainer and a dynamic public speaker. Blair's approach is one of high energy, intense and precise personal development and inspiration. His unique ability to get entire organizations to change behaviors quickly and achieve peak performance levels in a very short period is due to his high impact approach.

Blair is the author of the books: *SalesDogs: You Do Not Have To Be An Attack Dog To Be Successful In Sales* and *ABC's of How to Build a Business Team that Wins,* which are part of the Rich Dad's Advisors series. He founded and currently operates an international training firm that offers life-changing success strategies that have helped thousands increase their income through building championship sales teams.

Since 1987, Blair has worked with tens of thousands of individuals and organizations ranging from *Fortune* 500 companies to groups of independent sales agents, direct sellers and small-business owners to assist them in achieving extraordinary levels of sales, performance, productivity and cash flow. He is the Rich Dad Advisor who imparts the two most important skills required for success in business: sales and the secrets for building championship teams.

Blair was formerly the top salesperson for UNISYS and later a top performer in software sales, automated accounting sales and airfreight and logistics sales, both in the corporate world and as an entrepreneur/business owner. For the past 15 years, he has conducted thousands of public and private seminars with audiences ranging in size from 3 to 300 to over 10,000. His clients typically experience sales and income growth of 34 percent to 260 percent in a matter of a few short months depending on the industry. His work spans over 20 countries and across five continents. Overseas, he works extensively in Singapore, Hong Kong, Southeast Asia, Australia and around the Pacific Rim.

Robert Kiyosaki's Edumercial
An Educational Commercial

The Three Incomes

In the world of accounting, there are three different types of income: earned, passive, and portfolio. When my real dad said to me, "Go to school, get good grades, and find a safe secure job," he was recommending I work for earned income. When my rich dad said, "The rich don't work for money, they have their money work for them," he was talking about passive income and portfolio income. Passive income, in most cases, is derived from real estate investments. Portfolio income is income derived from paper assets, such as stocks, bonds, and mutual funds.

Rich Dad used to say, "The key to becoming wealthy is the ability to convert earned income into passive income and/or portfolio income as quickly as possible." He would say, "The taxes are highest on earned income. The least taxed income is passive income. That is another reason why you want your money working hard for you. The government taxes the income you work hard for - more than the income your money works hard for."

The Key to Financial Freedom

The key to financial freedom and great wealth is a person's ability or skill to convert earned income into passive income and/or portfolio income. That is the skill that my rich dad spent a lot of time teaching Mike and me. Having that skill is the reason my wife Kim and I are financially free, never needing to work again. We continue to work because we choose to. Today we own a real estate investment company for passive income and participate in private placements and initial public offerings of stock for portfolio income.

Investing to become rich requires a different set of personal skills – skills essential for financial success as well as low-risk and high-investment returns. In other words, knowing how to create assets that buy other assets. The problem is that gaining the basic education and experience required is often time consuming, frightening, and expensive, especially when you make mistakes with your own money. That is why I created the patented educational board games trademarked as CASHFLOW®.

Rich Dad Poor Dad

What the rich teach their kids about money that the poor and middle class do not. Learn how to have your money work for you and why you don't need to earn a high income to be rich.

The book that "rocked" the financial world.

J.P. Morgan declares *"Rich Dad Poor Dad* a must-read for Millionaires."
—*The Wall Street Journal*

"A starting point for anyone looking to gain control of their financial future."
—*USA Today*

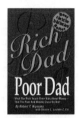

Rich Dad's CASHFLOW Quadrant

Rich Dad's guide to financial freedom. Learn about the four CASHFLOW Quadrants, and you will understand the most important keys to creating wealth.

The sequel to *Rich Dad Poor Dad, Rich Dad's CASHFLOW Quadrant* describes the four types of people who make up the world of business and the core value differences between them. It discusses the tools an individual needs to become a successful business owner and investor.

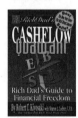

Rich Dad's Retire Young Retire Rich

A powerful personal story about how Robert and Kim Kiyosaki started with nothing, and retired financially fee in less than ten years. If you do not plan on working hard all your life, this book is for you.

If you're tired of the same old investment advice—such as "be patient," "invest for the long term," and "diversify"—then this book is for you.

Robert explains in detail the power of leverage. How to leverage your mind, your financial plans, your actions and most importantly, your first steps to becoming financially free.

You will learn rich dad's techniques using leverage to first build financial security and ultimately have the life you want.

Rich Dad Poor Dad for Teens

The Secrets About Money—That You Don't Learn in School! Learn how to have your money work for you and why you don't need to earn a high salary to be rich. Based on the bestselling book *Rich Dad Poor Dad,* this book is written for teens to cover essential information on how they can become financially free at any age. *Rich Dad Poor Dad for Teens* is packed with straight talk, side bars, and quizzes, this book will jump-start your personal success by showing you: how to speak the language of money, ways to make money work for you, tips for success—including "work to learn, not to earn," and games that help you understand the tools to keep money moving and growing.

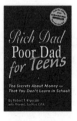

THE NEW YORK TIMES

writes:

"Move over, Monopoly®...
A new board game that aims
to teach people how to
get rich is gaining fans the
world over!"

WHY PLAY GAMES?

Play often and learn
what it takes to
get out of the Rat Race—
for good!

Games are **powerful learning tools**
because they enable people to experience
'hands-on' learning. As a **true reflection
of behavior,** games are a **window to
our attitudes,** our **abilities to see
opportunities,** and **assess risk and
rewards.**

Each of the CASHFLOW® games
creates a forum in which to evaluate life
decisions regarding money and finances
and immediately see the results of your
decisions.

TIRED OF THE SAME OLD FINANCIAL ADVICE?

Tired of hearing… "work hard, live frugally, cut up your credit cards, and get out of debt?"

READY TO HEAR WHY AND HOW THE RICH ARE GETTING RICHER?

The Rich Dad book series explains WHY and HOW in easy-to-understand terms so you can focus on and understand the keys to creating wealth and investment strategies of the rich. Each book will convey messages of hope and empowerment, enabling you to take control of your financial future.

"Never before has a single author or series of books—like Rich Dad—so dominated the best sellers lists. It's a feat unprecedented in the publishing arena."

—Larry Kirshbaum, Chairman *Time Warner Book Group*

TIRED OF THE SAME OLD FINANCIAL ADVICE?

BUT IT PAYS TO HAVE 'A' STUDENTS ON YOUR TEAM OF FINANCIAL ADVISORS

Rich Dad's Advisors are the 'A' students that advise Robert and his team—and who have played a key role in the Rich Dad success story.

Rich Dad's Advisors book series covers every key aspect of business and investing—from legal entities and intellectual property protection, accounting and tax strategies, sales and leadership skills to real estate investing and property management and investing in all asset classes.

For more information go to: www.richdadsadvisors.com

RichKidSmartKid.com

Money is a life skill—but we don't teach our children about money in school. I am asking for your help in getting financial education into the hands of interested teachers and school administrators.

RichKidSmartKid.com was created as an innovative and interactive Web site designed to convey key concepts about money and finance in ways that are fun and challenging… and educational for young people in grades K through 12. It contains 4 mini-games that teach:

Assets vs. Liabilities
Good Debt vs. Bad Debt
Importance of Charity
Passive Income vs. Earned Income

AND, schools may also register at *www.richkidsmartkid.com* to receive a FREE download of our electronic version of CASHFLOW for Kids at School.

How You Can Make a Difference

Play CASHFLOW® for KIDS and CASHFLOW 101 with family and friends and share the richkidsmartkid.com Web site with your local teachers and school administrators.

Join me now in taking financial education to our schools and e-mail me of your interest at *Iwill@richdad.com*. Together we can better prepare our children for the financial world they will face.

Thank you!

DISCOVER THE POWER OF THESE RICH DAD PROGRAMS:

- *Rich Dad's You Can Choose to Be Rich*
- *Rich Dad's 6 Steps to Becoming a Successful Real Estate Investor*
- *Rich Dad's How to Increase the Income from Your Real Estate Investments*

Step-by-step guides with audio components and comprehensive workbooks ensure that you can take the knowledge you gain and apply it to increasing the value and profitability of your investment portfolio.

ARE YOU WINNING OR LOSING THE GAME OF MONEY?

COMMUNITY NEWS FREE

As a Rich Dad Community Member, you'll receive Rich Dad's Community News FREE every month in your email!

- **Exclusive messages and tips** from Robert and Rich Dad's business team

- Notification of **events** that may be in your area

- News about **what Robert's up to** and **new developments** in the Rich Dad Community

For more information go to: www.richdadsadvisors.com

INSIDERS

Who says WATCHING TV & PLAYING GAMES will get you nowhere?

As an exclusive member of Rich Dad's INSIDERS, you will have access to all the features and benefits of Rich Dad's Free Community Membership—PLUS many added benefits:

- Exclusive invitations to Rich Dad events

- INSIDERS–only 800 Hotline

- Advance copy of Rich Dad's Community News–every month

- Access Rich Dad TV–24/7! Watch, listen, and learn from Robert and Rich Dad's business team through RDTV

- INSIDERS Blog–to journal your journey

- Analyze a Real Estate Investment with the online Real Estate Evaluation Tool

- Tips, articles, resources & more

The Perfect Business? Audio

In the exclusive audio interview, Robert Kiyosaki reveals his choice for the perfect business to help you retire rich. Prospects will discover successful strategies to create personal security and financial freedom. Excellent for recruiting! Approximately 20 minutes.

The Perfect Business! Video

Let Robert Kiyosaki show your prospects how direct selling can be their ticket to financial freedom. This exclusive video, shot in Robert's home, envelopes prospects with his revolutionary CashFlow Quadrant® wisdom, just as his rich dad shared it with him. Excellent for recruiting and follow-up. Approximately 11 minutes.

The Business School Book

With *The Business School For People Who Like Helping People* book, Robert Kiyosaki helps you build your network. Learn the Eight Hidden Values of a Network Marketing Business—Other than Making Money! Robert reveals one of the quickest ways to build a "B" Quadrant Business and why the word network is so powerful to the rich. Excellent for recruiting and distributor training. 144-page paperback book.

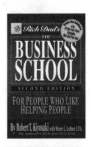

How To Be #1 In Your Business Book

In the follow-up to his best-selling Rich Dad's Advisor book *SalesDogs,* Blair Singer shares his unique perspective on how to build championship teams, regardless of your age, experience or gender. Learn how to build a #1 direct selling business...build great teams...build lasting relationships...and build a terrific home life for you and your family. Perfect for recruiting and distributor training. 96-page paperback book.

To order any of these products, check with your organization's tool supplier.